Cost-Effect[ive]
Home Upgr[ades]

Created and Designed by the Editorial Staff of Ortho Books

Project Editor
Barbara Feller-Roth

Writers
Morris and James Carey
The Carey Bros.

Assistant Writer
Tim Green

Photo Editor
Roberta Spieckerman

Principal Photographer
Geoff Nilsen

Principal Illustrator
Mitzi McCarthy

Ortho Books

Publisher
Richard E. Pile, Jr.

Editorial Director
Christine Jordan

Production Director
Ernie S. Tasaki

Managing Editors
Robert J. Beckstrom
Michael D. Smith
Sally W. Smith

System Manager
Linda M. Bouchard

Marketing Specialist
Daniel Stage

Distribution Specialist
Barbara F. Steadham

Sales Manager
Thomas J. Leahy

Technical Consultant
J. A. Crozier, Jr., Ph.D.

Address all inquiries to:
Ortho Books
Chevron Chemical Company
Consumer Products Division
Box 5047
San Ramon, CA 94583-0947

ISBN 0-89721-240-1
Library of Congress Catalog Card
Number 91-73777

Chevron Chemical Company
6001 Bollinger Canyon Road, San Ramon, CA 94583

Copy Chief
Melinda E. Levine

Editorial Coordinator
Cass Dempsey

Copyeditor
Rebecca Pepper

Proofreader
Deborah Bruner

Indexer
Trisha Feuerstein

Editorial Assistants
John Parr
Nancy Patton Wilson

Layout by
Cynthia Putnam

Composition by
Laurie A. Steele

Production by
Studio 165

Separations by
Color Tech Corp.

Lithographed in the USA by
Webcrafters, Inc.

Front Cover Collage
Roberta Spieckerman

Photographers
Names of photographers are followed by the page numbers on which their work appears.
R = right, C = center,
L = left, T = top, B = bottom.

Laurie A. Black: 30
R. Christman: front cover, middle column #1; 28
Michael Lewis: front cover, left column #2
Stephen Marley Productions: 82, 107BR
Geoff Nilsen Photography: front cover, left column #4; front cover, middle column #2 and #3; front cover, right column #1 and #2; title page; 3; 4; 5; 8; 10; 13; 16; 17; 29; 32; 33; 44; 48; 58; 59; 69; 74; 75; 83; 85; 86; 95; 96; 103; 105; 107L; 107TR; back cover TL, TR, and BR
Joyce OudkerkPool: 55
Kenneth Rice: front cover, left column #1; 39; 41; 42; 43; 71; back cover BL

Homeowners
Maria Arapakis
Jo Alice and Wayne Canterberry

Manufacturers
Closet Dimensions: front cover, left column #2
Marvin Windows: 14
Miracle Method: front cover, left column #3; 64
Velux-America, Inc.: 54; 58; 59; 103
Wenco Windows, Mt. Vernon, Ohio: 80

Special Thanks To
Joan Annett and Ed Osborn
Anne Gilderslieve and Steve Flannas
Nancy and Jack Holtzapple
Susan and Brendan McEntee

Architects/Contractors/ Designers
Carey Bros. Remodeling, Pittsburgh, Calif.: front cover, left column #4; right column #1; 8; 83; 107L; 107TR
Linda Fotsch, South Point Sausalito Design and Construction, Sausalito, Calif.: front cover, middle column #2; title page; 29; 44; 48; 69
Glen Jarvis Architects, Berkeley, Calif.: front cover, middle column #3; front cover, right column #2; 3; 4; 5; 10; 13; 16; 17; 32; 33; 74; 75; 86; 95; 105; back cover TL, TR, BR
Joint Enterprises, Christopher Osborn, El Cerrito, Calif.: front cover, middle column #3; 4; 5; 85; 95; 96
Kahn Design Associates, Berkeley, Calif.: 85; 96
Loretta Kelly Korch, Interior Design, Palo Alto, Calif.: 58; 59; 103
Susan Hill-McEntee/Interior Design: 3; 13; 16; 32; 74; back cover TL and TR
Jan Newman Design, Burlingame, Calif.: 55
Don K. Olson, AIA, Sausalito, Calif.: front cover, middle column #2; title page; 29; 44; 48; 69
Jared Polsky & Associates, Larkspur, Calif.: 32
The Steinberg Group, Rob Steinberg Architect, San Jose, Calif.: 58; 59; 103

Front Cover
You can make your home more livable and more salable by investing your time and money in the most cost-effective upgrades, as illustrated by these small, medium, and large home improvements.

Title Page
The arched entry to the dining room is gracefully echoed in the opening for the French doors, the pass-through to the kitchen, and the kitchen window. The bullnose trim of the openings softens their edges.

Page 3
A hallway that is inviting and wide enough to display artwork is gained by removing closets that had run the length of the space, by installing recessed lighting, and by adding a skylight.

Back Cover
Top left: A built-in home entertainment center conceals the television and other electronics, allowing the focal point of this remodeled living room to be the fireplace. It was refaced, and a period mantel, found in a salvage yard, was installed.

Top right: The entryway to this home was given definition and grace by adding a new columned arbor, which allows the garage to relate to the house rather than upstage it.

Bottom left: A new undercounter oven and small cooktop helped to transform this awkward corner into a handsome tiled cooking area.

Bottom right: Adding a new bay window in the basement was the most cost-effective way to gain an extra bedroom in this house. The foundation is a natural window seat and base for bookcases.

Cost-Effective Home Upgrades

PLANNING HOME IMPROVEMENTS

Getting the most for your home-improvement dollar is a primary concern if you are planning to fix up your home, whether you are merely refinishing a bathroom light fixture or remodeling the entire kitchen. As a homeowner or a prospective home buyer, you probably have several projects in mind. If you are like most people, you have neither the time nor the resources to accomplish all of them. This book is designed to help you prioritize your wish list of home improvements by presenting information on the payback, safety, and convenience of dozens of typical upgrades. Where to begin, who to call, how to prepare, when to do it, and tips on how to do it—it's all here. The emphasis is on moderately priced projects you can do yourself, but major improvements that you will likely delegate to a professional are also included.

Adding slope to the flat roof of this home resulted in a spacious, airy living room with a dramatic vaulted ceiling, Palladian window over the front door, and gracefully descending stairway from the new second-story addition.

WHERE TO BEGIN

Planning is the secret to home-improvement success. This section will help you set priorities to determine which project is the most important and most cost-effective, make a master plan to estimate costs and prevent construction conflicts, develop detailed plans, determine a budget, and decide how the work will be done and who will do it.

Getting an Overview

An upgrade can be as easy and uncomplicated as regular home maintenance. Buffing a porcelain bathtub can compensate for years of wear and lost luster. Such face-lifts can make your bathroom more pleasant to use as well as being cost-effective if you are selling your home.

Major improvements can also bring a high return on your home-improvement dollar. In addition, spending $20,000 to remodel a bathroom can be more cost-effective than moving when you consider that the combined costs involved in selling your house, buying another, and moving can equal 10 percent of the sales price of your house.

Monetary return is a significant consideration in every home-improvement project. This return includes resale value, prevention of costly repairs, and reduced upkeep costs. For example, it is more expensive to install a ceramic-tile shower over a mortar-bed backing than it is to glue ceramic tile directly to wallboard; however, mortar adds strength, smoothness, and superior waterproofing. The additional 50 percent spent on mortar makes the improvement last three to five times longer. Projects that are not built to last diminish the return on your initial investment and may be several times more costly to repair.

Details are also important. Painting a door and leaving the old knob, or replacing the bathroom floor covering and reusing a worn-looking heat register can result in an unattractive, unfinished appearance.

A Showcase of Cost-Effective Upgrades

The house illustrated here is showcased at the beginning of each chapter, where each of these upgrades and many more are shown and called out in detail. See page 18 for the front view listing all exterior upgrades. See pages 35, 60, 76, 89, and 98 for detailed illustrations and listings of upgrades in every room in the house. The most significant upgrades are listed here.

1. New siding
2. New window trim
3. New bay window
4. New front entry
5. New garage door
6. Arched pass-through to dining room
7. French doors to new deck off dining room
8. Built-in cabinets in dining room
9. Entertainment center in living room
10. New fireplace
11. Pop-out wall for breakfast nook
12. New garden window in bathroom
13. Whirlpool tub
14. Twin sinks
15. Open staircase to refinished attic
16. Built-in closets in bedroom
17. Entertainment center in bedroom
18. French doors to new deck with spa off bedroom
19. Window seat with bookshelves
20. Garage work space

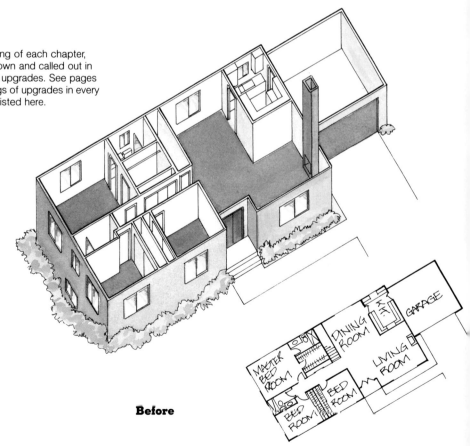

Before

Not every remodeling project will provide a big return on cash invested. The justification for some projects, especially the more luxurious ones, will largely be increased personal pleasure and comfort. However, even luxurious renovations can be done cost-effectively. With proper planning you can meet your needs with minimal confusion and maximum cost-efficiency.

Studying the Neighborhood

When planning, the first consideration is the context of the home. It's important not to overimprove or underimprove for the neighborhood. Overimproving a home can price it out of the market at resale time. In fact, the most expensive house in a neighborhood is often difficult to sell. Whether you plan to sell your home or stay in it, however, you would be wise to keep an eye on local home values to help you prioritize home improvements.

Getting to know the value of the homes in a particular neighborhood involves a little detective work. One easy method is to scan the real estate ads in local newspapers or look for a list of real estate transactions and the selling prices. (Some papers carry them.) Another method is to hire a real estate appraiser, although this can be expensive. The best alternative is to contact a local real estate agent. Most will provide a detailed market analysis, usually at no charge.

In a healthy real estate market, it's a good rule to avoid improvements that will raise the value of a home to more than 20 percent above typical values in a neighborhood. In a sluggish market it's best not to push the remodeled value of the home above typical values at all. For homes in mixed-value neighborhoods, it's smart to keep remodeled values no higher than the top values, no matter what the condition of the real estate market.

As the following examples show, the math is easy.
□ In a healthy market the owner of a $180,000 home in a neighborhood of $220,000 homes should set a cap on improvements at $84,000, for a remodeled value of $264,000 ($220,000 + 20 percent).

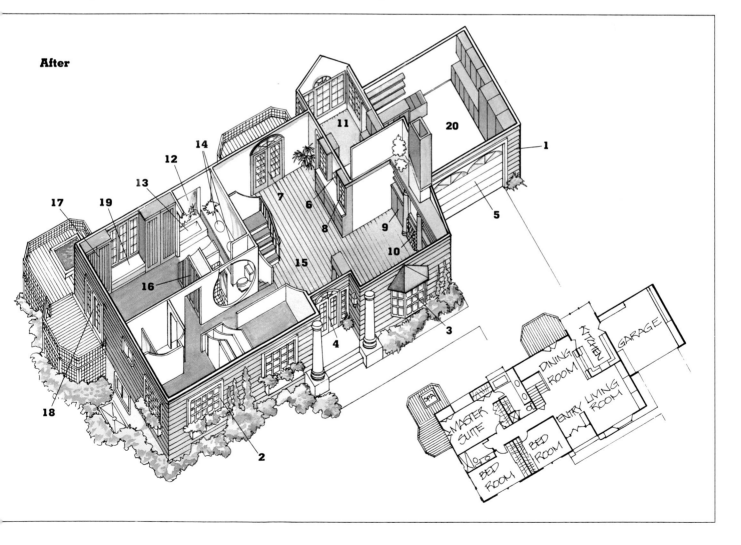

After

7

☐ In a sluggish market the owner of a $180,000 home in the same neighborhood should spend no more than $40,000, for a remodeled value of $220,000.

☐ In a mixed neighborhood where the top home value is $220,000, the owner of a $180,000 home should invest no more than $40,000, regardless of the market.

These guidelines mean that in many neighborhoods it is smart to resist the temptation to put in granite kitchen countertops, build a fifth bedroom, or make other expensive improvements if they will increase the value of the home beyond a reasonable level for the neighborhood.

On the other hand, not improving a home enough can also make it difficult to sell. If typical homes in a neighborhood have two-and-a-half bathrooms, it's a good idea for the owner of a one-bathroom home to add at least one more bathroom to bring the home up to a level similar to the others in the neighborhood.

It is also important to try to match the quality of the other houses in the neighborhood. If your kitchen cabinets, countertops, and floor coverings do not match the quality found in other houses in the neighborhood, the most cost-effective upgrade would be to make similar improvements.

Try to resist improvements that are very personal in nature. Even though you may want a bright pink polished-granite entry hall, dark brown wallpaper, or an indoor shooting range, many people probably will not, and they won't be willing to pay for it. These types of individualized improvements, in many cases, lower the value of a home or even scare off potential buyers.

Setting Priorities

By setting priorities, you make sure that the most important and financially sensible jobs get done first. Although setting priorities may seem like an obvious first step, many homeowners plunge headlong into projects, spending money and time on low-priority improvements when more important jobs are left undone.

For example, a family room addition is thought by many to be an attractive project that boosts home value. It can be potentially worthless, however, if the master bathroom of the home is outdated and its wiring is dangerously substandard. With a list of priorities, it's easy to see that a new family room in this house is a "could," a new master bath is a "should," and rewiring is a must. Adding a family room to this house would be like putting new tires on a car with a bad engine.

Prioritizing Projects

When you are balancing a file folder filled with ideas against a limited home-improvement budget, some projects may end up at the bottom of the list or be dropped altogether. That's the idea of setting priorities—to help ensure that the "musts" get done before the "shoulds" and that the "shoulds" get done before the "coulds." The following is a list of priorities in order of importance.

1. Safety

Threats to family health and safety, violations of fire or building codes, and structural weaknesses should be given top priority. Do not undertake other improvements until these problems have been corrected. Safety-related improvements include replacing an old patio door made of nontempered glass, replacing dangerous electrical wiring (especially aluminum wiring), applying nonslip decals to the bottom of the bathtub, and reinforcing a broken or sagging structural member, such as a roof rafter or a floor joist. Also included in this category are security improvements, such as fire alarms, childproof cabinet latches, and exterior lighting.

An older ranch-style home with a shallow-sloped roof was given new life with contemporary doors and windows, a steeper roof added to the central portion of the house, and a master bedroom wing on the right side of the house, in which the former enclosed outdoor barbecue was remodeled as the new bedroom fireplace.

Combining Priorities

The most cost-effective improvement is the one that combines the most priorities—in this case, a new roof.

Priority List
New Roof
① *reduces maintenance*
② *improves appearance*
③ *cures leak by chimney*
④ *meets new fire retardant material codes*
⑤ *increases safety*
New fence
② ④ *improves appearance*
③ *Paint Exterior*
④ *reduces maintenance*
⑤ *improves appearance*

2. Cost Control

Any project that would help decrease utility bills, lower maintenance costs, or prevent a large repair in the future falls into the category of cost control. Such improvements include installing double- or triple-pane windows, adding insulation and weather stripping, and repairing or replacing a leaky roof.

3. Basic Repairs

Often, seemingly minor improvements have as much impact as major upgrades on the overall appearance of a house and the family's daily life. Most of the jobs in this category are simple fix-its or cleaning projects that take a little elbow grease, such as patching wall cracks, eradicating mildew, caulking a shower, removing countertop stains, cleaning and buffing a kitchen sink, caulking around window and door frames, refinishing a light fixture, and replacing a toilet seat. Other more expensive examples include replacing broken appliances, bolstering a sagging garage door, and replacing worn floors.

4. Appearance

The fourth priority consists of projects that improve the appearance, or curb appeal, of a home. Some people may argue that these improvements are fairly costly compared to the direct, functional benefits they provide. It is difficult to measure the impact of, say, new exterior shutters. But to consider them unnecessary because they have no actual function can be shortsighted. Like general repairs and maintenance, changes to the exterior or interior of a home for appearance's sake can make a big difference, especially if the home will be for sale in a year or two. Improvements in this category include installing a new front door, painting the exterior, replacing floor coverings, adding crown molding or chair rail, replacing plastic tub surrounds with ceramic tile, adding a greenhouse window in the kitchen, and installing a skylight.

5. Function

Improvements that make the home function more efficiently and that have a direct impact on daily life make up the fifth category of priorities. A large variety of improvements fall into this category, and they cover a wide price range. A functional improvement in the kitchen could range from a new dishwasher to a complete redesign and remodeling. Functional improvements elsewhere in the house would include an extra bathroom for the children, basement storage shelves, a larger garage, and extra clothes closets.

6. Life-Style

Life-style improvements tend to be expensive but are some of the most effective and fun to do. Examples include adding a family room, expanding the master bath to handle the morning needs of two working people, turning a spare bedroom into a study, adding a deck, and installing a whirlpool bath or a home spa.

7. Luxury

Luxury improvements fall into the "want" category. They can be done cost-effectively, but they are usually so user specific that the return on investment can be very poor, especially if they result in an overimprovement for the neighborhood. But if the money is available, and if you have taken care of higher priority home improvements, you may be able to justify such luxury improvements as an indoor pool, a billiards room, a sauna, walnut woodwork, or a kitchen full of commercial-grade appliances.

Combining Priorities

A single improvement, in many cases, can take care of more than one priority. In fact, that should be the goal. For example, a garden window can lend beauty to a room; if it is a double- or triple-pane window, it can also be more energy efficient than the window it replaces. Another example is a repainted house exterior, which adds curb appeal and also protects the exterior surface. The illustration above shows how a new roof combines the most priorities of the three possible upgrades listed; hence, it is the most cost-effective.

Making a Master Plan

Planning improvements to a home is like putting together a jigsaw puzzle; seeing the big picture helps you to know how the pieces fit together. A master plan provides a way to look at the big picture.

Seeing the Big Picture

The first consideration when making a master plan is how projects will fit into the overall home-improvement scheme. The master plan does not have to be very detailed; this is not the time to select paint colors or choose between wood and vinyl windows. Instead, you decide in general what improvements will be done—their scope, their location, and their timing.

A master plan enables you to make smart improvements that won't have to be torn out in the future. It will help you to develop a preliminary long-term home-improvement budget, which helps in setting up a savings or borrowing plan.

A master plan can save a lot of headaches and money down

the road. Suppose that your home-improvement wish list includes a ceramic-tile tub enclosure (priority 4, appearance) and, a few years later, a complete remodeling of the bathroom (priority 6, life-style). Without a master plan, it would be impossible to know how the tub enclosure will fit into the eventual renovation, or whether it will fit at all.

Because a master plan is general in nature, it won't say, for example, whether the floors in the future remodeled bathroom will be covered with sheet vinyl, carpet, or ceramic tile. But it will say that the new bathroom should include a whirlpool tub. That's important to know, because the tub will require a special pump-access door and possibly more space than the old standard-sized bathtub around which the original tub enclosure was constructed.

As another example, let's say that a deck and a new family room are on your wish list. Both projects are priority 6 (life-style), but the deck—a relatively

inexpensive improvement—is scheduled to be done right away, and the family room—an expensive improvement—is scheduled for three years in the future. With a master plan, you could design the deck to fit around the future family room so that the deck wouldn't have to be changed extensively or completely rebuilt when the family room is added.

Setting and Getting Value

The second consideration when making a master plan is the value of specific improvements.

Although most people remodel to make their house more enjoyable and more functional rather than specifically to increase its value, few families stay in one house forever. Therefore, resale value should be kept in mind when planning home improvements, because at resale time the value of individual improvements becomes vitally important. The table on page 11 gives an alphabetical listing of popular home-improvement projects and their value at resale.

This new bedroom addition was designed to bring the outdoors in and convey an airy brightness with skylights, a vaulted ceiling with ceiling fan, and a window seat overlooking the garden.

Even when nationwide statistics show that homeowners are receiving an excellent overall return on home-improvement investments, the resale value of specific improvements can vary greatly. Extravagant, unusual, and overly personal upgrades usually return only a fraction of their cost, whereas the upgrades that home buyers like the most will return most, if not all, of their cost.

It's important to balance your needs against the return you can expect on your investment dollar. Set up your own criteria, and be clear on what you want, keeping in mind that resale value is the value other people put on improvements. When planning improvements, try to think like a home buyer.

What do today's home buyers want? Mostly, they want bright, modern kitchens and large, luxurious bathrooms. Several consumer organizations and magazines periodically publish lists ranking home improvements by payback value. The left column of the table on page 10 is an example of a list taken from a magazine in 1990. The list in the right column—by a national homebuilders' association—ranks the top nine remodeling projects by popularity. Keep in mind that these polls can serve as guidelines, but they should not be the sole basis for your decisions.

A home improvement doesn't have to be expensive to catch a home buyer's eye. Of the first five improvements listed in the right column, only one (remodeling a bathroom) could be considered a major improvement. And, as the table above shows, projects such as

Home-Improvement Costs and Paybacks

Home Improvement	Average Cost	Return Percentage
Bathroom addition	$11,000–$35,000	50–200%
Bathroom remodeling	7,600–18,000	70–75%
Closet expansion/organizing system	1,000–2,000	80–100%
Deck	5,700–9,500	60–75%
Fireplace	4,300–7,700	50–100%
Garage addition	16,000	50–60%
Hardwood floors	4,700	60–70%
Insulation	1,500–2,500	65–70%
Interior face-lift	5,300	70–85%
Kitchen remodeling (major)	24,000–44,000	60–100%
Kitchen remodeling (minor/face-lift)	10,000–18,000	70–85%
Landscaping	15,200	50–60%
Master bedroom remodeling (major)	32,000–65,000	80–90%
Roof replacement	7,000–20,000	50–60%
Room addition	20,000–75,000	60–80%
Siding	8,500–28,000	65–75%
Skylight	3,500–6,500	60–70%
Sunroom	15,000	55–70%
Swimming pool	30,000	0–40%
Window replacement	10,000–20,500	55–70%

increasing the energy efficiency of a home (particularly an older one), adding closet space, or putting in a skylight make a big difference to buyers and, in the end, may bring back their entire cost.

Looking at Cost Versus Value

The third consideration when making a master plan is cost. The table above is an alphabetical listing of popular home-improvement projects, their cost, and their payback at resale. Although these values were calculated in 1990, you can use them as a benchmark. Since costs vary widely from area to area, the price ranges shown here are based on national averages. The wide range is due to three variables: labor cost (which varies regionally),

the size of the room, and the degree of detail executed in the upgrade. The return percentages reflect the value of the improvement if the house was sold within one year after the improvement was completed. The percentages are affected by the following factors.

□ The value of the home relative to others in its neighborhood. Do the improvements add value, or do they just bring the home up to par?

□ The condition of the real estate market. The value of home improvements rises and falls with the ups and downs of the market.

□ The years since completion of the upgrade. In some, but not all, cases, resale value decreases over time.

□ Style and taste. What was popular last year might not be as popular next year.

□ Regional differences. Some improvements are valuable because of climate, tradition, or local preferences.

Rating the Upgrade

All of the upgrades listed in this book are divided into three groups: small, medium, and large. Small projects are those that can be completed in a day or two for less than $500. Medium projects can be completed in two to six days for $500 to $2,000. Large projects cost more than $2,000 even though some can be completed in a day or two. Included in this last category are major remodeling projects, which in many cases can cost more than the original price of the house.

TIME FOR ACTION

Now that your master plan is finished, it's time to get to work. Sticking to the priorities you've established and following the master plan will ensure that the most important and financially sensible jobs get done first.

Creating Specifications and Building Plans

You will use the master plan to create exact project specifications and a set of plans.

Specifications are important because the price and quality of products such as doors, windows, floor coverings, and faucets vary widely. It is important to find out why price differences exist (usually because of differences in quality and the number of features), decide on what is important for your purposes, figure out how the products will fit into the final project, and select a specific manufacturer and model for each product.

This is where knowledge of home improvements becomes extremely valuable, especially for large projects. You can hire architects, designers, and design-and-build remodeling contractors to create specifications from scratch, but this can be expensive. By performing the basic investigation yourself and making eliminations and selections before meeting with a professional, you can save a lot of money. If you plan on doing the project yourself, the same sort of investigation is essential.

The first step in creating a list of product specifications is to gather information, such as brochures, about different products. Then make the specification list, including such information as make, model, color, style, texture, size, and so forth. This list can then be used by an architect or a designer— or by you if this is a do-it-yourself project—to produce a set of detailed building plans. A complete set of building plans is especially crucial on all large projects, regardless of who will perform the work.

Using Resources

A wealth of information exists on home-improvement and remodeling projects. The library is a good source of free information from both books and magazines. Well-stocked bookstores will likely have dozens of illustrated home remodeling publications. There are many fine publications by Ortho Books and others—some encyclopedic in their approach, others concentrated on specific areas, such as tile, kitchen remodeling, and so on. Numerous home-improvement magazines exist; some emphasize design, others construction and technique. A variety of residential building and decorating magazines is widely available in supermarkets and drugstores. Cost-estimating guides can also be useful; look for them in the local library or ask a contractor if you can borrow some. Most construction and remodeling trade associations produce a variety of informational booklets with tips designed to help you get the most for your remodeling dollar. There are also several building schools around the country where you can learn how to build or remodel your home. See page 108 for a list of resources.

Doing It Yourself

For many homeowners, the first, and seemingly the least expensive, option for a home-improvement project is to do the job themselves. This works best on small- and medium-sized improvements, but if you enjoy working on your home, and you have the necessary skills or the time to learn them, it is possible to do even large projects yourself.

Be aware, however, that there is no guarantee that doing a large project yourself will save money, especially when you apply a dollar value to your time. If you do decide to undertake a large project yourself, be sure that you are willing to perform a great deal of physical work and that you have the self-discipline to plug away at the job, no matter how long it takes.

Unlike small remodeling projects, which can be completed in a weekend, bigger jobs can take weeks or even months to complete. As such, they require careful planning to avoid delays and to minimize disruption in your life. It may be helpful to think of the project as a second job: Set a work schedule and stick to it.

Even if you work at it faithfully, a large do-it-yourself project can take much longer than if you hired professionals. For most working people, the only time available for do-it-yourself projects is in the evenings and on weekends, and in a typical workweek that doesn't add up to very many hours. It's important to know, too, that building inspectors and most suppliers work regular business hours, and so someone will have to be home during the day when they are expected.

A less time-consuming option is to perform only parts of the large projects yourself and to hire professionals to do the rest. The following are a few tips if you choose that alternative.

☐ Do the work of the highest-paid construction professionals (usually electricians and plumbers) if you have the skills.

☐ Do labor-intensive and costly jobs, such as hanging wallboard, insulating, and painting.

☐ Do general labor, such as demolition, daily cleanup, and refuse and materials hauling.

You can also act as your own general contractor and hire subcontractors—carpenters, plumbers, electricians, wallboard finishers, cabinet installers, painters, tilers, and so on. Acting as your own general contractor is a big job that is loaded with responsibility. You must be well organized, persistent, and clear about the details of the project. You must be available to spend hours on the telephone and on the job site. You must be comfortable negotiating with subcontractors and suppliers. You must be articulate, firm, and patient, and be willing to stay out of the way and, when appropriate, get involved. You must be skilled in handling money, and you must make payments promptly and keep a budget. You are responsible for reporting the wages of salaried workers to the IRS, withholding state and federal taxes, and paying the employer's share of those taxes. You must also carry workers' compensation insurance.

As general contractor, you are responsible for the schedule. It is the key to a successful job; subcontractors depend on it. If the job isn't ready for their part when scheduled, subcontractors must reschedule. It could be days or weeks before they are able to come back, sometimes at extra cost. And that delay can scramble the project schedule even further. Yet in every project delays are to be expected, and as the general contractor you must stay on top of them, adjust the schedule, and inform the subcontractors as far in advance as possible.

If you decide to be your own general contractor, it is wise to add 20 percent to the project budget as a contingency. For example, if you expect the project to cost $40,000, plan on reserving an extra $8,000 to cover unforeseen costs and inexperience. Contractors usually allot 10 percent for this purpose, and even experienced contractors sometimes find that 10 percent is insufficient.

Hiring a Building Team

For most people, the best way to make home improvements that are cost-effective and to spend money wisely is to hire professional help, especially for large projects or those they don't feel comfortable doing themselves. In the long run, hiring a professional can often save money, as well as time and the aggravation of living with partially completed do-it-yourself projects. The key is to find an honest, reliable professional. The time you spend locating one can be the deciding factor in whether this option is cost-effective. A little detective work, some common sense, and a few simple guidelines will help you to compile a list of good-quality professionals from which to choose. The following sections describe how to choose the potential members of the building team.

A former narrow kitchen was given a feeling of spaciousness and light with the addition of skylights and an island divider to replace the previous wall between the kitchen and family room. The tongue-and-groove ceiling in the family room has been retained; upgrades in the remodeled kitchen include a new tile back splash and random plank oak flooring.

Selecting an Architect or a Designer

Many architects and designers are specialists in remodeling, which is different from new construction and takes specific design talent. The best way to select this member of the team is to look at examples of his or her work and talk to past clients. A reputable professional will be happy to provide the necessary addresses and telephone numbers. It is also important to talk to several current references who have had a similar type of project designed. Some professionals may be good at interior design but less successful on exterior alterations.

Architects must pass an exam to be registered in the state in which they work. In addition, they may be registered by the National Council of Architectural Registration Boards. Registered architects may also be members of the American Institute of Architects (AIA). See page 109 for sources of information.

Designers handle work similar to that of architects, but they cannot call themselves architects because they have not been licensed or registered by the agencies previously mentioned. Designers are generally less expensive to hire than architects and are often used for projects such as small room additions and kitchen and bathroom remodeling projects.

Because many building agencies require that an architect or a structural engineer approve the plans submitted for building permits, when designers are hired to create plans that involve structural changes, they must hire an architect or a structural engineer to stamp the plans with their registered seal. This is perfectly acceptable. In many cases, especially large projects, licensed architects are also required to have their work approved or structurally designed by a licensed civil or structural engineer.

Most of the rules that apply to hiring a contractor can be used to find a good architect or designer. See below.

Selecting an Interior Designer

Interior designers deal more closely with furnishings, decorations, color, and style than architects or designers. You can hire an interior designer individually or in conjunction with an architect. Better designers are registered by the American Society of Interior Designers (ASID) or the International Society of Interior Designers (ISID). See page 109 for addresses.

Selecting a Remodeling Contractor

An increasingly popular alternative to hiring an architect or a designer is to seek the assistance of a design-and-build remodeling contractor, or a design-and-build team (an architect or a designer and a remodeling contractor who regularly work together). In a team, the designer or architect works with design features such as light, ventilation, and traffic flow, whereas the remodeling contractor provides input about mechanical difficulties and other construction-specific details, current costs, and product availability.

There is a difference between a remodeling contractor and other types of general contractors. Remodeling contractors specialize in renovating existing structures, generally ones where people are living. Therefore, the remodeling contractor must be highly skilled in communicating what's happening as each event occurs. The remodeler must also be skilled in dealing with older types of construction as well as current building methods and codes and approved methods of conversion. General contractors who build custom homes and subdivisions are not trained to deal with older building methods, and are usually not experienced in performing construction when people are living in the house while the work is being done.

Your project will be more pleasant for everyone involved if the remodeling contractor you select is skilled in business, is familiar with and follows the law, and knows how to give a fair and correct price. A careful search for a professional can help you avoid incompetent, unprofessional contractors. The following checklist will help you select a reputable remodeling contractor.

☐ Verify the name, address, and telephone number of the contractor. If the address given is a post office box, the contractor may be hiding the actual business location.

☐ Ask for financial data and references. It is wise to get the same information from a remodeling contractor that a bank would need to process and approve a loan for a

Sliding French doors opening onto a new brick patio add charm and appeal to this older home. The chair rail with wallpaper below it was added to enhance the traditional look.

prospective borrower. One excellent way to get this information is to ask a local bank for a credit application form and have the contractor fill it out. Then check all the references, including suppliers, subcontractors, and past customers.

It's important to make sure that the remodeling contractor you select is financially solvent. Lien laws in many states may leave the homeowner responsible for paying the subcontractors if the contractor fails to do so, even if the homeowner has already paid the contractor for the work.

☐ Ask for the names and telephone numbers of past and current customers for whom the contractor has performed similar work, and call them to see if they were satisfied with their projects. It is also wise to visit several of the remodeling contractor's completed jobs. A telephone opinion may suffice, but seeing is believing.

☐ Make sure that the contractor is licensed (where required), carries liability and workers' compensation insurance, and is bonded. Get copies of all license, insurance, and bonding certificates. Verify the current standing of the remodeling contractor with the issuing agencies. A list of contractor licensing boards for each state is on page 109. A call to the Better Business Bureau in your area can also help you determine whether the contractor is in good standing. (Check the local telephone book for the number.)

☐ Comparison-shop by obtaining two or three bids for the project. Bids will usually vary

by as much as 8 to 12 percent between reputable remodeling contractors. When the range is greater than that, be extra cautious. Usually, low bidders have omitted something, are using faulty estimating techniques, are planning to take shortcuts, are working with poorly detailed plans, or don't have experience in bidding on your type of job. They may also be bidding low to get the job, planning to tack on an increase during the project. A tip: If anything doesn't make sense, ask the contractor to explain it.

☐ Don't automatically choose the lowest bidder—remember that price is only one of the selection criteria. Higher bidders may be using higher-quality materials. Make sure that the bids are detailed enough to permit you to compare them. The bid should list all the work required; work not listed—even providing a light bulb—will probably not be performed.

☐ Consider the contractor's professionalism, demeanor, and interpersonal skills. Since he or she will be in your home for many hours every day, it is important that the person you hire be pleasant to be around.

Reviewing the Contract

Once you have selected a remodeling contractor, the contract is the next step. The following checklist will help you make sure that all parties are treated fairly.

☐ Get everything in writing. The contract documents should include the contract, a copy of the plans, a copy of the specifications, and copies of all other documents related to the project. The contract should spell out exactly what the contractor will and won't do, and it should include financial terms, starting and finishing dates, warranty information, and a payment schedule. (Be aware that in many states it is illegal to pay for the work in advance.) Make sure that the contract allows you to withhold a reasonable percentage (usually 10 percent) of the total payment until the job has been completed satisfactorily.

☐ Insist on building permits where required. A permit sets the inspection process in motion and ensures that the construction is done in accordance with the building codes. Building codes are interpreted differently from city to city, but all are designed to promote the health and safety of the occupants of the building. No other job requirement is more important than permits.

☐ Make sure that the remodeling contract includes an arbitration clause. Arbitration can sometimes help to resolve disputes without the need to resort to costly lawsuits. To learn more about arbitration, contact the nearest office of the American Arbitration Association.

☐ Make sure that the remodeling contract specifies that changes to the work be approved in writing by both the owner and the contractor. This prevents arbitrary changes from being made at arbitrary prices.

☐ Make sure that the remodeling contract includes standard clauses concerning governing law in the state where the contract is written, who will pay attorney fees in the event of a dispute, and what measures can be taken by a party if the other fails in its responsibilities under the terms of the contract.

☐ Read every word in the contract and attached documents, and don't sign anything that seems confusing, incorrect, or unclear. If you are in doubt about anything, it may pay to have an attorney review the contract documents.

☐ Don't sign a certificate of completion for the job before it has been inspected by the appropriate authorities and has been completed according to the contract.

Preparing for Disruption

Even the neatest and most experienced remodeling contractor can make a mess of the house. Remodeling is dirty work. Dust will be everywhere. Expect it and plan for it, and the mess won't be so difficult to deal with. Be aware that during construction you may temporarily lose the use of a toilet, shower, dishwasher, or stove, and you may not have hot water or a clothes closet for a day or two. Plan for these interruptions. Focus your thoughts on how beautiful your home will look once the work is done.

THE EXTERIOR

The old saying that first impressions are lasting ones is especially true about a home. An attractive, well-maintained exterior says a lot about the occupants of a house. Whether you are interested in selling your house or fixing it up to enjoy it yourself, an attractive exterior adds value and comfort. A good paint job on the siding and decorative trim and a nicely landscaped yard make the house look better and also make it a more pleasant place to be. Well-maintained gutters prevent water damage. A well-maintained surface on the driveway and walkways makes the house safer and also makes it look cared for. Plaster and mortar that are in good condition make the house more watertight, reducing the chance of water damage and improving the appearance of the house as well. These are just a few of many small and medium upgrades you can do to keep the exterior of your house safe and in good condition.

Most realtors agree that curb appeal is more important in selling a house than any of its other features. Although this book isn't just about fixing up a house to sell it, people do move frequently—sometimes when they least expect to—and a well-maintained home commands the best price because it shows well.

A new columned arbor is the handsome link that relates the garage to the house and transforms the entryway to this home.

SMALL EXTERIOR UPGRADES

Maintenance is the most cost-effective way to deal with the exterior of the house, because most exterior features, such as siding, roofing, and masonry, are expensive to replace. Many exterior maintenance projects are inexpensive and easy. Like all the small projects listed in this book, these upgrades cost less than $500 and can be completed in a day or two.

Improving Exterior Lighting

For the money, exterior lighting enhances a home and landscaping more than most other exterior improvements.

The least expensive and easiest system to install is a low-voltage system. It is also more energy efficient and less expensive to operate than a standard system, because power is stepped down from the standard 120 volts, in most cases to 12 volts. The system consists of individual light fixtures and a transformer that plugs into a standard outlet, usually with a timer. Because the connecting wires carry only low voltage and are waterproof, they can be strung above ground or buried below ground.

Solar-powered systems are also available. They are more cost-efficient than standard electric fixtures to install and operate (they don't use electricity), which more than offsets their higher purchase price.

Light switches that detect motion and body heat have come down in price since they originally appeared on the market. Any movement in the area at which the detector is aimed will turn on the light. As long as the movement continues, the light will stay on. The switch also includes an adjustable timer that will shut off the lights automatically after no motion has been detected for a specified length of time. Carrying out the trash or walking between the garage and the house at night are both safer with lights that come on automatically.

Repairing Electrical Wiring

Improper wiring can cause fires. All exposed exterior wiring should be encased in a proper electrical conduit (a metal pipe).

Ideally, exposed wiring should be moved into the attic or basement area. It is safer there, and moving it indoors avoids unsightly wires and pipes on the exterior. In most cases, running wiring in the attic or basement area is less expensive than using conduit on the exterior, since the metal pipe, the connectors, and the tools required to work with conduit are expensive.

Exterior Upgrades

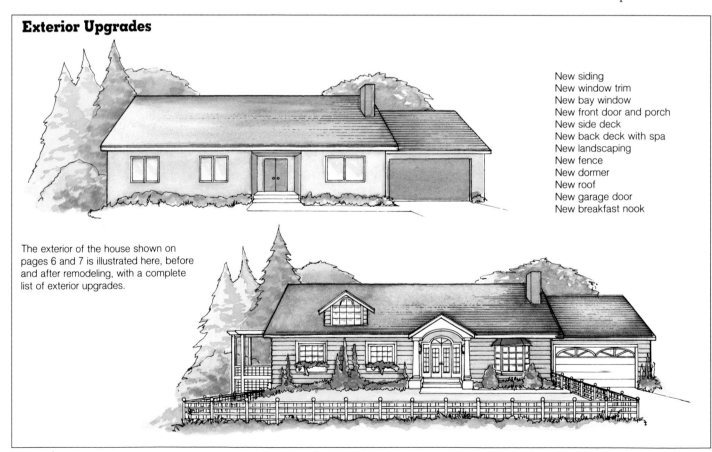

New siding
New window trim
New bay window
New front door and porch
New side deck
New back deck with spa
New landscaping
New fence
New dormer
New roof
New garage door
New breakfast nook

The exterior of the house shown on pages 6 and 7 is illustrated here, before and after remodeling, with a complete list of exterior upgrades.

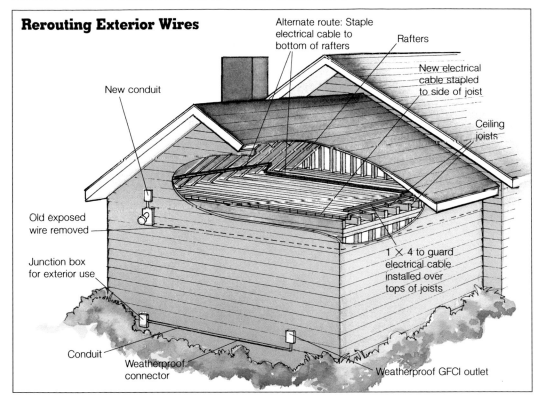

Rerouting Exterior Wires

New conduit

Old exposed wire removed

Junction box for exterior use

Conduit

Weatherproof connector

Alternate route: Staple electrical cable to bottom of rafters

Rafters

New electrical cable stapled to side of joist

Ceiling joists

1 X 4 to guard electrical cable installed over tops of joists

Weatherproof GFCI outlet

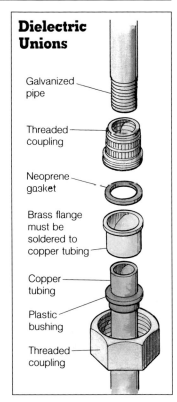

Dielectric Unions

Galvanized pipe

Threaded coupling

Neoprene gasket

Brass flange must be soldered to copper tubing

Copper tubing

Plastic bushing

Threaded coupling

If hiding the wire is not possible, then running a conduit is the only smart choice left. A 25-foot length of exposed wire can be made safe in an afternoon. Use waterproof boxes and wire made for use inside conduit. Never use electrical tape to join and protect wire connections. Electricity can arc through the tape across two wires (or a wire and the junction box) and could cause a fire. Special wire connectors are made to prevent this from happening

Place a weatherproof junction box at the point where the wire exits the house. Run electrical conduit from the box to the place where the wire ends. At that point, connect another junction, plug, or light box to the conduit. String new wire from the first junction box to the last one.

Although the National Electrical Code regulates electrical installations, the code can be superseded by municipal laws. It is wise to consult local building officials for advice prior to starting an electrical project.

Repairing Faucets

Leaky faucets can waste a lot of water. Faucet gaskets are usually the culprit. They have a tendency to hum; the dried gasket vibrates as water passes over it. You can replace these gaskets in about half an hour at very little expense. A faulty faucet valve can cause reduced water flow. For just a few dollars more, you can replace the entire hose bibb or faucet in about the same time it takes to replace a gasket.

Replacing a faucet is simple. First, turn off the main water inlet valve. Then unscrew the old faucet (counterclockwise) with two pipe wrenches or a large pair of channel-type pliers. Having the proper wrench or pliers makes this an easy task. Finally, wrap the threads of the replacement faucet with pipe joint tape, or paint them with pipe joint compound, and screw the faucet into place.

Unclogging Sewer Drains

Root growth and grease build-up are the two most difficult intruders to remove from a sewer drain. If a 25-foot snake won't clear the drain, chances are that one or both of these problems exists.

Unclogging such obstructions is a task for professionals.

Cleaning sewer drains improperly can damage the pipes beyond repair, and replacement can cost thousands of dollars.

If you are thinking of having a sewer-cleaning company do the work, require them to guarantee that they will replace any pipe that they damage during the cleaning process. Ask them to give a price for unclogging the drain before they start the work.

Replacing Clogged Water Pipes

Clogged water pipes, evidenced by reduced water flow throughout the house, not just in one fixture, cannot be cleaned. They must be replaced.

Galvanized pipe should be replaced with copper pipe; it

lasts longer. Use dielectric unions where the new copper pipe connects to old galvanized pipe, to prevent an electrolytic reaction (the deterioration of metal that results when dissimilar metals come into contact with each other in the presence of water).

Repairing Cracked Stucco

The most important part of repairing cracked stucco is blending the repaired cracks into the existing surface. The type of caulk to use depends on the thickness of the crack. For cracks less than ¼ inch thick, use a paintable silicone caulk. It shrinks less than others and remains pliable enough to withstand movement as the joint expands and contracts with changes in temperature.

Apply the caulk to the open joint, force it into the crack with a putty knife, and then use a dampened sponge to match the surface of the caulk to the stucco surface being repaired. Avoid using too much caulk; a wide caulked joint can be as unsightly as the original crack.

For cracks larger than ¼ inch thick, use a stucco-patching compound. For maximum adhesion, thoroughly clean the crack of all debris and loose stucco. Then mix and apply the patching compound according to the manufacturer's directions.

Keep in mind that patching compound only fills the crack—it does not bond the broken edges of the stucco—so that any movement of the stucco, due to settling or earthquakes, will probably cause a crack to open up again.

Repairing Wood Siding

Wood siding that is split or cracked can be mended with exterior-grade patching compound. For major damage, use epoxy-based wood fillers. With the proper technique, the repair will be invisible. Before mending wood siding with patching compound or epoxy, it is important to ensure that the damaged siding is securely fastened. If not, it should be renailed and the new nail holes patched.

To mend smoothly finished siding, use a paint scraper to expose bare wood. Then, with a 2-inch-wide putty knife, push patching compound into the crack. At first, while the freshly spread putty is still wet, it will bulge at the crack. As it dries it will shrink and recede into the crack. Each coat of patching compound should be applied and then sanded when dry. Two or three applications will be necessary. Applying the compound too thick in an effort to hide the crack with one coat can result in a lot of unnecessary sanding. To prevent the first coat of patching compound from pulling out of the crack as you are wiping it onto the wood with the putty knife, dip the cleaned blade of the putty knife into a container of water and rewipe the puttied surface.

To mend rough- or resawn-surfaced siding, follow the technique for mending smooth wood, but use a wire brush instead of sandpaper on the patch. The wire bristles will cut irregular grooves into the dried patching compound, making the patch less visible.

Replacing Damaged Wood Siding

Siding that is too damaged to be repaired with patching compound can be patch-replaced. This involves removing the damaged siding and replacing it with new material. When a sheet of plywood is damaged, the entire piece must be replaced, but the removal is easy. Simply use a cat's paw (nail remover) to pull out all the nails that hold the plywood in place, use the removed plywood as a pattern to cut a new piece, patch the siding paper with an approved patching compound, and then nail on the new piece of plywood.

Plank siding is not as expensive as plywood to repair because the amount of wood required for a patch can be restricted to the damaged area. However, the process is more labor intensive and can damage the siding paper.

To make the repair, cut out the damaged plank with a circular saw. Adjust the blade depth to $1/16$ inch less than the thickness of the siding, which is usually ¾ inch thick. After cutting the material, remove the nails with a cat's paw, and then remove the siding and use it as a pattern to make the replacement piece. The process for replacing plank siding is the same as for plywood siding. Seal all joints—new and old—with exterior caulk.

If a plumbing pipe penetrates the siding to be replaced, turn off the water, cap the supply pipe, drill the hole in the siding at the pipe location, install the siding, replace the cap with the pipe, and turn on the water. Trying to cut around a hose bibb will leave a large, unsightly hole in the siding that will make the repair look unprofessional. Follow a similar procedure for electrical devices.

If the siding on an entire side of the house must be replaced, this project could be a medium to large upgrade.

Repairing Roof Leaks

Roof leaks are not expensive to repair, but finding the location of the leak can be a challenge. For example, water dripping from the living room ceiling could be coming from a leak over the kitchen. Water has a tendency to travel along the underside of the roof sheathing and rafters before finally dripping down into the house. Water stains on the rafters indicate that a leak exists, but they do not necessarily indicate where the leak is on the roof.

Finding a leak is not difficult, but it can be time-consuming; hence, hiring a contractor to find the leak can be expensive. To find a leak yourself, use a hose to spray small areas of the roof (one 5- or 6-foot-square area at a time) heavily with water. The smaller the area you spray, the better your chance of pinpointing the location of the leak. Spray for about ten minutes in each area; less time may not be sufficient for the water to pass through to where it can be seen. If no attic exists, and there is a layer of interior finish material such as wallboard, remove it and expose the roof rafters. Water can puddle atop the wallboard for 15 to 30 minutes before beginning to drip through.

For a sloped roof, start at the overhang (the lowest point) and work toward the ridge (the highest point), being careful not to spray water up under the shingles. Sloped roofs are not completely watertight and can leak if water is forced underneath the shingles.

Caution: Be extremely careful when walking on a sloped roof, especially when it is wet.

Once you have found the leak, replace the shingle or shingles causing the problem, or use roofing mastic to patch the underlying roofing felt. If metal flashing is found to be the culprit, liquid solder is the appropriate patch material.

Caring for Wood Roofs

Keeping wood shingle and shake roofs clean and water-resistant helps deter leaks. Wood shingles and shakes are easily and quickly damaged by the sun's ultraviolet rays. Sun and wind evaporate the natural oils found in the wood, allowing it to absorb water. The wood then expands, causing the shingles to split and cup (curl).

Keeping the roof clean also inhibits the growth of mildew and other fungi. Although moss, leaves, and other debris don't damage wood roofing material, they trap moisture that can cause damage. The moisture provides an ideal habitat for fungal growth, such as soft rot, which quickly deteriorates wood.

The easiest way to clean a roof is to power-wash it. The best time is in the fall, before heavy winter weather begins. Be careful not to force water underneath the shingles. Every third year, follow the washing with a light spray of shingle and floor oil. Be sure that it is specified for roof applications and meets local fire requirements. The oil keeps water from traveling deep into the wood and helps prevent cupping and splitting by keeping the shingles soft, pliable, and water-resistant. Mixing a small amount of paint pigment, available in a range of colors and sold in tubes, into the oil will ward off damage caused by ultraviolet rays.

Caution: Be extremely careful when walking on an oiled sloped roof. When oiling a roof, it is wise to be tied to the other side of the roof with a sturdy safety rope.

Cleaning is an important part of roof maintenance. To prolong the life of your roof, it is also important to replace shingles that are beyond repair and to treat the roof with a preserving chemical. This should be done every five years. Once the roof is clean, replace split and damaged shingles. Finally, apply a chemical to the entire roof to preserve and protect the shingles. Either an oil-based or a water-based solvent can be used to carry the chemical. In dry climates the oil-based solvents are better. The chemical used to help preserve wood shingles is an approved pesticide (such as copper naphthenate), so take care to apply it properly. Paint pigment is purchased separately and added to the chemical to hide the green cast left

by the pesticide and to blend the new shingles into the rest of the roof.

Using a reputable roof maintenance company is an alternative to doing it yourself. It is important to hire a firm that offers a five-year unconditional guarantee. Roof maintenance done correctly every five years can save 40 percent over the cost of replacing a roof. Painting roof shingles may void any warranties and is not recommended.

Cleaning Gutters and Downspouts

Gutters and downspouts are designed to prevent rainwater from falling onto the ground near the foundation of the house. This preventive measure is important because wet soil adjacent to a foundation undermines the support needed for the foundation to remain stable. Downspout drain leaders should extend at least 3 feet from the foundation before draining onto the ground. Many communities require downspouts to drain into an underground piping system that carries all rainwater into a local storm drain system.

As a point of information, the storm drain system and sanitary sewer system are usually separate entities. Sewer systems are supposed to route waste to treatment plants; storm drain systems usually drain into nearby rivers, streams, or settling ponds, moving flooding to a safe place outside the community.

If gutters and downspouts aren't kept clean, water will overflow onto the ground adjacent to the foundation, and the foundation may shift as a

---

Repairing a Bowed Shake

1. Split out ⅛" to ¼" splinter, then nail on each side of split

2. After removing shingle, cut nails that held it

3. Fit new shingle into gap and nail in place; cover nails with roofing cement

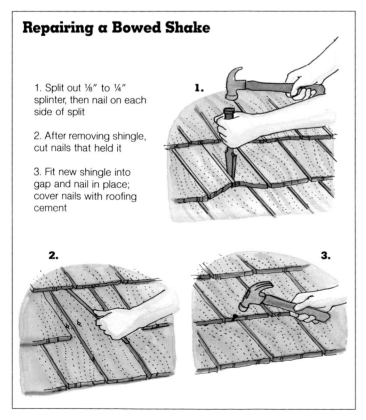

Checking for Moisture Problems

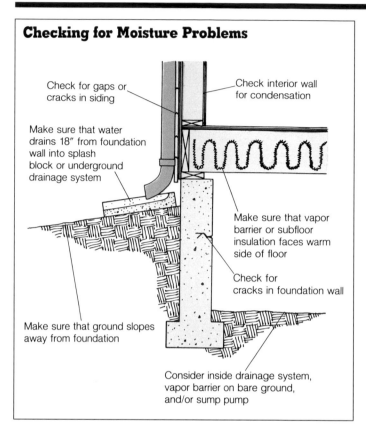

Check for gaps or cracks in siding

Check interior wall for condensation

Make sure that water drains 18″ from foundation wall into splash block or underground drainage system

Make sure that vapor barrier or subfloor insulation faces warm side of floor

Check for cracks in foundation wall

Make sure that ground slopes away from foundation

Consider inside drainage system, vapor barrier on bare ground, and/or sump pump

Constructing a Strongback: An Alternative to Straightening Ceiling Joists

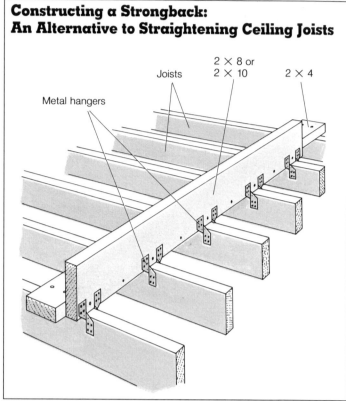

Joists

2 × 8 or 2 × 10

2 × 4

Metal hangers

---

result. When the house shifts, walls crack, floors buckle, and windows and doors don't operate smoothly. Preventing this problem is as easy as sweeping and hosing out gutters and downspouts at the end of fall, and adding leaders to the end of the downspouts to carry water a minimum of 3 feet away from the foundation.

Solving Grading and Drainage Problems

If floors are squeaking or buckling, windows and doors are not operating properly, or plaster is cracking, the problem may originate with an unstable foundation.

A house is only as stable as its foundation, and a foundation is only as stable as the soil on which it rests. When the

moisture content of the soil is excessive due to poor drainage, the entire house is affected.

Proper grading is essential for good drainage. All surfaces (dirt, concrete, brick, and so on) within 30 inches of the perimeter of the house must slope away from the foundation at ¼ inch of fall for each linear foot of travel. Otherwise, water will settle around the foundation and can cause it to shift.

On flat building lots (as opposed to hillside property), proper grading is usually all that is needed. However, in some situations an underground French drain can be used to carry water away from the foundation (see illustration). Even on flat in-town lots, the ground must be graded to slope slightly so that water will run off toward municipal storm drains.

Controlling Structural Pest Damage

Eliminating earth-to-wood contact is an almost cost-free project that can reduce the possibility of rot and termite infestation.

The Uniform Building Code requires earth to be at least 6 inches away from any wood in the home; the Federal Housing Administration requires 8 inches. There are two reasons for eliminating earth-to-wood contact: Earth in contact with wood (or any cellulose material) attracts termites and related pests and gives them direct access to a food source; and wet earth in contact with wood promotes fungus growth, which causes wood to rot. It begins when the wetness of wood reaches 20 to 30 percent.

To eliminate earth-to-wood contact, remove all earth (including planting bed areas and cellulose debris) within at least 6 inches of all wood structures. Most stucco exteriors have wood behind them near their base and should be dealt with like wood siding.

If a fence butts up against the exterior wall of the house, add flashing in the form of a thin layer of galvanized sheet metal between the fence and the house, to keep termites from traveling from the fence into the exterior siding and then into the structure.

If no earth-to-wood contact exists, finding termite trails is easy. Termites avoid light and prefer to travel from the earth into a home through tunnels that they create from mud. It is wise to inspect the exposed subarea frequently for mud tunnels. They are about the size

Fixing a Sagging Garage Door Opening

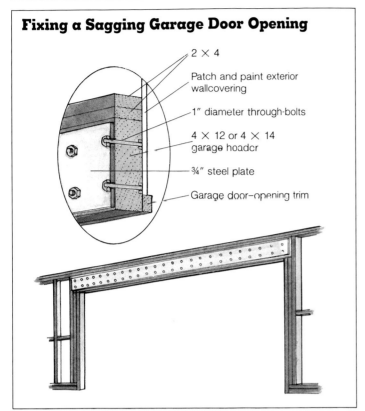

- 2 × 4
- Patch and paint exterior wallcovering
- 1" diameter through-bolts
- 4 × 12 or 4 × 14 garage header
- ¾" steel plate
- Garage door–opening trim

Fixing a Sagging Floor

Saw old floor joist so that it can be jacked up and nailed to new straight joist

---

of a pencil and can be found against the inside of the foundation wall between the ground and any nearby wood. If you find termite tunnels, call a specialist in structural pest control to exterminate the termites.

Fixing Deteriorating Posts

Wood posts that sit directly on concrete, such as posts that support patio or porch covers, can deteriorate after several years. The post absorbs rain and irrigation water, fungus damage begins, and the post starts to rot at the bottom.

Repair is easy. First, brace whatever the post is supporting with temporary posts; then cut off the lowermost inch of the post with a handsaw, and

paint the cut with wood preservative. Reconnect the post to the concrete with a sheet-metal post base (with spacer). Move the cut post out of the way, attach the post base with concrete nails, and then place the spacer in the base, followed by the post. Remove the temporary brace, and finally nail the top of the post base securely to the post. The spacer inside the post base supports the post far enough above the concrete to deter future capillary action, keeping the post dry and extending its life.

Fixing Sagging Garage Door Openings

In an older home a sag may occur in the garage door header, the horizontal wood timber above the door that

makes up the top of the opening. A sagging header is caused by either the weight of the roof or the weight of the floor above the garage door. Once the header has sagged, it must be either replaced or raised and braced with a steel plate.

As a do-it-yourself project, replacement is by far the more cost-effective option because this project is labor intensive (see also page 98). If done by a professional, this would be a medium upgrade.

Use temporary supports to hold the structure in place while the header is being replaced. Cut all nailed connections, using a reciprocating saw with a metal-cutting blade. Remove the header and use it as a pattern for its replacement. The replacement timber should be the strongest grade of lumber available—select structural.

If the work will be done by professionals, adding metal bracing can be more cost-effective than replacing the header, because less labor is involved. If you choose bracing, contact a structural engineer to determine the thickness of the steel plate and the number and size of the bolts to be used to make the repair with a steel-plate brace.

Fixing Other Sagging Framing Members

Floor, ceiling, and roof framing members can also sag after being in place for many years. The fibers tear at the lower side of the horizontal framing member as a result of the weight from above. With roof rafters and ceiling joists, the weight of the roof can cause this to happen. With floors, furniture or load-bearing walls can be the culprit.

Once a horizontal framing member has sagged and completely dried out, its shape is almost permanent. To repair it, cut the sagging member at its lowest point, raise it to a point slightly higher than its original position, and then sister (glue and nail or bolt) a new framing member alongside it.

When sistering a new horizontal framing member to an old one, it is wise to use a larger size for the sistered piece when possible; it will be stronger and resist sagging more effectively. For example, you would sister a 2 by 8 floor joist with a 2 by 8, 2 by 10, or 2 by 12 if space allowed.

Upgrading Concrete Flatwork and Blacktop

Walkways and driveways with cracked concrete or potholed blacktop can be unsightly and dangerous. Damage usually occurs when the earth below heaves or shifts, a condition usually brought on by extreme drying, as from a drought, by excessive moisture, or by alternate freezing and thawing.

If no drought exists, chances are that excessive landscape irrigation water or wet weather are causing the damage. Once it occurs, the additional openings in the surface allow even more moisture to permeate the ground below. Patching compounds, which are formulated to expand and contract with changes in temperature at the same rate as the concrete or blacktop, can help to prevent

Repairing Damaged Concrete

Replacing Broken Concrete

1. Undercut any edge of solid concrete

2. Fill with concrete mix, then finish and let cure

Repairing Hairline Cracks

1. Brush out all loose material, then caulk

2. Smooth off excess with your thumb

Repairing Cracks or Holes

1. Undercut edges, then clean and dampen

2. Fill with patching mix, trowel smooth, and let cure

continued water seepage. Be aware, however, that patching compounds are not permanent and will require continued maintenance. In addition, it may be difficult to match the original color.

Concrete is cracked beyond repair when patches don't hold, existing cracks widen, new cracks develop, and major shifting occurs. If you want to replace the concrete, have a soils (or geotechnical) engineer recommend a method of replacement. For example, before pouring the new concrete, digging

out 6 to 8 inches of earth and replacing it with compacted rock could reduce the chance of future cracking. Installing a grid of ½-inch steel rebar and using a mix of concrete that contains more cement than usual might also help.

Blacktop sealer protects blacktop against weather damage. To repair small cracks in blacktop, brush out any loose matter and fill the cracks with butyl cement. Smooth the top with a putty knife. Fill large cracks and holes with blacktop

patching compound, packing it down with a shovel or tamp. Lay a board over the area, and drive on it with your car to compact it completely. See illustration at right.

Patching Concrete Foundations

Foundation cracks can be unsightly but may not indicate serious damage. When you notice cracks (hairline or otherwise), it is best to consult a structural engineer to ensure that a serious problem does not exist.

Repairing Holes in Blacktop

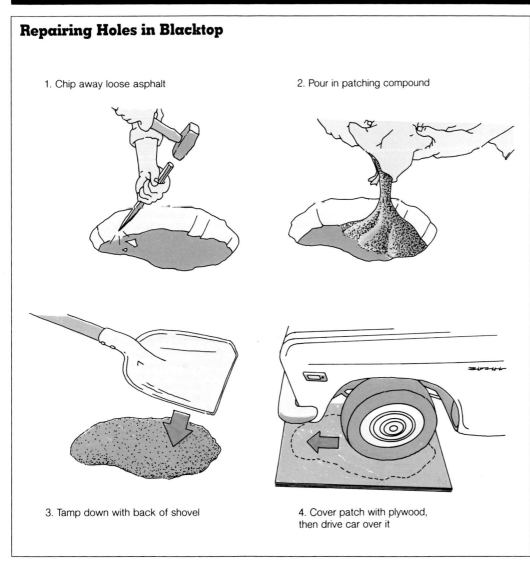

1. Chip away loose asphalt

2. Pour in patching compound

3. Tamp down with back of shovel

4. Cover patch with plywood, then drive car over it

For do-it-yourself cosmetic repairs of cracks that are not serious, use latex concrete patching compound. The easiest type is already mixed, although patching compound is also available in powdered form that you mix with water.

Maintaining Exterior Caulk

Maintaining caulk on the exterior of the house is an easy, inexpensive face-lift that can save thousands of dollars. Caulk is used to create a water seal at joints, especially around windows and doors. Eventually, the caulk dries out, causing it to shrink and crack. Water can then reach framing members, which can result in serious fungus damage.

The best kind of caulk for the exterior of the house is paintable silicone. Silicone caulk was not available when older homes were built; latex caulk, which dries out, was used then instead.

The most obvious caulked joints in a house are wood-framed windows where the glass fits into the frame and is sealed with glazer's putty. Unlike other caulk, glazer's putty becomes extremely brittle after it has been in place for several years. Since removing the brittle putty could result in cracked window panes, simply rough up the old putty with a wire brush, and then apply new putty with a putty knife. If the old putty has been painted, remove all paint before applying the new putty.

Glazer's putty has a linseed-oil base, and therefore is water-resistant. However, it will last longer if it is painted.

Insulating Walls, Ceilings, and Floors

You can make your home more comfortable and reduce heating and cooling costs by adding insulation to walls, ceilings, and floors. This upgrade is not done to the exterior of the house (although adding wall insulation can be done from the outside), but it affects the building envelope and is therefore considered an exterior upgrade.

Insulating floors and ceilings that are accessible by a crawl space or an attic is an easy do-it-yourself project. Insulation is relatively inexpensive to buy and simple to install.

Batt insulation is the best type. It comes in rolls in widths designed to fit between framing members that are either 16 inches or 24 inches on center. You can cut the insulation to length or to odd widths with a utility knife or a pair of scissors.

Foil-backed insulation is not recommended, because condensation occurs at the foil layer, which can cause water damage. Paper-backed or backless insulation is better. If you use paper-backed insulation, place the paper toward the inside of the house.

In the attic, simply lay insulation in place; pierce the paper backing if you are installing it over existing insulation. In the basement area, position insulation between the floor framing members, and hold it in place with flexible rods, baling wire,

25

or fiberglass netting nailed to the bottom of the floor framing members.

Use caution when working with fiberglass insulation to prevent the minute glass particles from entering the body or becoming embedded in the skin. Wear a breathing mask to keep from inhaling the particles, use goggles for eye protection, and cover the entire body (including the head) with clothing. Use duct tape to seal clothing at the neck, wrists, and ankles.

Note: For walls and for ceilings where no attic exists it is best to have a professional install insulation. This project qualifies as a medium upgrade; special equipment is required to blow cellulose insulation into the wall and ceiling cavities. Keep in mind that fiberglass insulation is more resistant to moisture than cellulose insulation and if installed properly will last longer.

Controlling Air Infiltration

Insulating without controlling air infiltration is like trying to bake without closing the oven door. Infiltration control includes weather-stripping doors and windows, sealing penetrations between the basement area and the living area above, sealing penetrations between the attic and the living area below, and installing gaskets or sealing all penetrations in exterior wallcoverings.

Infiltration control is even less expensive than insulating and is easier to do. Canned spray foam, scraps of sheet metal, and rubber switch-plate

and outlet gaskets are the materials used. For example, in the attic or basement area, you can seal large holes at pipe or duct penetrations with a scrap of sheet metal; seal smaller openings with expanding spray foam. To seal heat-register covers in walls, floors, or ceilings, remove the cover, fill the gap between the supply duct and the wallboard with foam, and replace the cover.

To find penetrations in a previously insulated attic, use a lighted candle. Air escaping from the living area below exerts pressure as it passes through small holes into the attic—sometimes with enough force to extinguish the candle but always with enough to cause the flame to flutter. Be careful when performing this test, and carry along a small fire extinguisher.

A surprising amount of air can enter a house through switch plates and electrical outlets. Installing gaskets under these covers is an easy, inexpensive, cost-effective upgrade that will help to eliminate air infiltration. The gaskets are available at hardware stores. Simply remove the switch plate or outlet cover, install the gasket, and replace the cover. You can reuse the original screws that hold the cover in place—the rubber gaskets are thin.

Although any kind of weather stripping is better than none at all, weather stripping that is attached with nails or screws is far superior to the preglued stick-on type. For doors, the most effective (and most expensive) weather

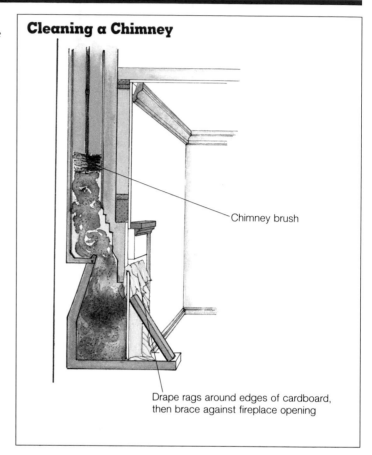

Cleaning a Chimney

Chimney brush

Drape rags around edges of cardboard, then brace against fireplace opening

stripping is the interlocking type. Some companies specialize in the installation of interlocking weather stripping.

Doors and windows should be weather-stripped where the fixed frame meets a moving part (on the top, bottom, and both sides). Double doors should also be weather-stripped where the two doors meet in the middle.

Cleaning Chimneys

Fireplaces that are used frequently, especially those that are fueled with resinous wood such as pine or fir, cause a greater creosote buildup in the chimney than less frequently used fireplaces or those in which hardwoods, such as oak,

ash, or walnut, are burned. Creosote is a by-product of combustion that adheres to chimney walls. It is flammable and under certain conditions can be explosive. It should not be allowed to build up in the chimney for long periods of time.

A chimney sweep can thoroughly inspect and clean a chimney in a few hours. See the illustration above to do it yourself. If cracks are found in the masonry, have a licensed or certified professional do the repairs. Do not use the fireplace until the repairs are completed, since cracked masonry can cause a house fire.

MEDIUM EXTERIOR UPGRADES

Whereas painting and cleaning inside the house are small upgrades, because they can be confined to one room, such upgrades on the exterior often involve the entire house, so they are bigger projects. Medium upgrades cost between $500 and $2,000 and take from two to six days.

Power-Washing the Exterior

Realtors agree that a freshly painted house does more for curb appeal than any other single project. However, painting may not be necessary to create a fresh look. Power-washing the exterior might be all that is needed. Since power-washing is the first step in preparing for exterior house painting, it's cost-effective to make the investment in time and equipment rental to find out whether cleaning can be a less expensive alternative to painting.

Because power-washing is 90 percent labor intensive, it can be done by a homeowner for a tenth of the cost of hiring a professional. As a do-it-yourself project, power-washing an 1,800-square-foot house could take two to three days. If the paint stays on without streaking, and oxidation (chalky powder) comes off, you have saved the cost of house painting.

Power washers force water through a fine nozzle with compressed air. The more powerful the stream of water, the more effective the cleaning. The water force at the tip of the most powerful (and professional-type) washers is approximately 3,000 pounds per square inch at a rate of flow of 6 gallons per minute. When shopping for this type of machine, ask for a 6/3,000 ("six three thousand") pressure washer.

Caution: Be extremely careful when using high-pressure spraying equipment. The force of the water can shatter glass, gouge soft wood, and drive metal particles into the skin.

Repainting the Exterior

If power-washing alone does not restore the exterior, painting is needed. Eighty percent of a good paint job lies in proper preparation. Even the best-quality paint won't last on a poorly prepared surface. Loose paint left by the power-washing should be scraped and sanded, voids should be puttied, then a primer should be applied. The primer creates a bond between the old layer of paint and the new one and also helps to fill voids and hide flaws.

Always paint the base color first and the trim color second. In most cases it is easiest to rent an airless sprayer to apply the paint. Do not do this on a windy day; wind can cause overspray to travel several hundred feet. It is important to brush or roll the sprayed-on paint before it dries. This process, called backbrushing or backrolling, forces the paint deep into the pores of the surface, adding years to the life of the paint job.

Installing Energy-Efficient Windows

Energy-efficient windows make a home more comfortable and lower heating costs by reducing heat loss. They are most cost-effective to install in climates where heating and cooling costs can be excessive. A wide variety of windows is available, including vinyl- and aluminum-clad wood windows, solid vinyl windows, double-pane glass (a requirement in many states), and gas-filled thermal windows (which reduce sound transmission).

The insulating value of a window is expressed in U-value. A good U-value for a window is U-4 or U-5. The lower the U-value the better the insulating quality. (This is the opposite of the R-value used to rate wall insulation, where a higher R-value indicates better insulating quality.)

Wood windows generally insulate and deaden sound better than metal ones, but unclad wood windows must be painted from time to time and are more expensive to purchase. In addition, condensation is more likely to occur at the frame of a metal window, and if ventilation isn't sufficient, water damage and mildew will result at areas adjacent to the frame. A few metal window manufacturers offer metal-framed windows whose frames are thermally efficient; however, they are not in wide use and are expensive.

There are three basic methods for replacing windows. The method you use significantly affects the final appearance, cost, and water-resistance of the new window.

The least expensive method is to rivet or screw a new frame to the old one. The rivets are unattractive and are a dead giveaway that replacement has occurred. The joint is sealed with caulk, which is not as watertight as flashing.

The second method involves cutting out the old frame and installing a jamb-mounted frame. Again, caulk is used instead of flashing, but the chance for an effective seal is better because the connection is not at the exterior surface.

The best replacement method is to remove the exterior wall covering and install the replacement window in the same way that the original window was installed—properly connected to the siding paper for an effective seal. Initially, this is the most expensive alternative, but preserving the water-resistant integrity of the exterior wall is more cost-effective in the long run.

Unless you have a lot of experience, leave window replacement to a professional. An improperly flashed installation may leak, which can cause extensive damage.

Controlling Heat Gain and Loss

Sunlight streaming into the house through windows, doors, and skylights is welcome during cold weather, but the reverse can be true on a hot summer day.

You can use window coverings to control heat gain and loss. They should be adjustable so that they can be closed to keep out the sun in summer and opened to allow it to pass through in winter. A simple canvas shade can be used with almost any type of window dressing. Miniblinds are more expensive but provide the same versatility. It is wise to avoid permanent window films and nonremovable awnings, since they can reduce heat gain in winter.

On the sunny side of the house, trees can also be located to control heat gain and loss. Deciduous trees can shade a house in summer and let the sun through in winter, when they lose their leaves. Coniferous trees, most of which retain their needles the year around, keep the house cool in summer and are also a good wind block in winter. Tall conifers can, however, block light in winter, when the sun is low in the sky, and should thus be situated carefully. With some species the lower branches can be pruned to allow the winter sun to pass through. In cool, damp climates, prune trees with thick foliage to allow sunlight through and to reduce condensation and mildew growth.

Improving Appearances

An attractive exterior enhances the livability of a house for its current residents and also makes it more appealing to prospective home buyers. Typical improvements include fences, decks, patios, a new front door, shutters, window boxes, decorative walkways, and even an interesting mailbox. Depending on the size and complexity of the project, this can be a small or a medium upgrade.

Adding Fences and Decks

A fence can enhance the landscape of your home by adding privacy, deterring damage from neighborhood pets, and diminishing noise. If you are planning to sell your house in a neighborhood where most of the homes have fences, it is wise to have one also. Private yards may not be popular in every community, but in areas where fences do exist, buyers will expect to see one. Although you may not be able to recoup the entire cost of installing a fence when you sell your house, not having one could deter a sale.

Some communities require building permits for fences, as well as for decks and patio covers, and have regulations concerning maximum height and proximity to the street. It is wise to check with the local building department.

Decks and patios enhance the livability of a home by providing outdoor entertaining areas. The design possibilities are endless, as evidenced by the wide range of books and magazine articles devoted to the subject. The return on this investment is better with elaborate decks and with those that are well maintained.

Decks and all other wood exterior additions should be built with wood that will resist damage by sun, rain, and snow. The best materials are redwood, cedar, cypress, and lumber that has been pressure treated. The natural resins in redwood, cedar, and cypress deter damage by structural pests and resist water damage far better than pine or fir. Pressure-treated materials should be approved for use on decks, since some of the chemicals used are poisonous.

Be aware that covered patios do not constitute additional square footage of living area. The return on investment for covering a porch or patio is relatively poor, so it should be done primarily to satisfy personal need.

Replacing the Front Door

A handsome front door helps create a favorable first impression of a house.

The main cost factor in door replacement is the door itself,

Curb appeal is created with plantings in the center of the driveway and a white picket fence, both appropriate to the style of the house and repeating its white trim.

not the installation, although some types of door handles can be several times more expensive to install into the door than others. The least expensive door-handle installation requires boring four holes: two from the exterior of the door to the interior and two from the edge of the door through to the first two holes. With the proper-sized drill bits, you can do this job in less than 15 minutes. On the other hand, some door handles require that a deep pocket be chiseled into the door. This process can sometimes take hours, and the door can be easily damaged by someone unskilled in using a chisel.

There are two methods of door replacement: retrofitting a new door to fit the existing frame or replacing both the door and frame.

Retrofitting is the least expensive method, but you should be aware of two things: Since a doorjamb (frame) is rarely exactly square, a replacement door should be trimmed to match the old door, and the door and the jamb should be finished (painted or varnished) so that they complement each other. A marred door jamb will detract from a new door.

Replacing both the door and the frame is far more expensive. The frame need not be replaced if the old one is in good condition. A varnished door in a painted frame is perfectly acceptable. However, if the budget permits, a varnished door in a varnished frame looks more impressive.

High-quality doors are made from solid wood, such as oak, ash, and mahogany, which will withstand abuse from all types of weather. A solid door deadens sound better than a hollow one and is more difficult for burglars to break down.

If you want to buy a raised-panel door, it is wise to select one with a few large panels rather than several small ones. The former has fewer places to fail because it has fewer connections. Years after the door has been installed—especially if proper maintenance has not been performed (regular painting or varnishing), the panel-to-door joints usually begin to separate. Properly maintaining the door to protect it from the elements will also lessen the chance of the panels splitting.

An older home sparkles with two new decks, French doors, and new lighting fixtures. The slate squares laid down over the wood decking seemingly continue the inside to the outdoors.

L ARGE EXTERIOR UPGRADES

The upgrades in this section have the most significant impact on home value and appearance. If you are trying to make an outdated house look modern, the upgrades listed here may be for you. Large upgrades cost more than $2,000, although some may take only a day or two.

Installing Stone and Masonry Veneers

Solid masonry walls are expensive. However, brick or stone can be applied as a veneer over stucco or wood siding, adding richness to the exterior at a more reasonable cost than that of building solid masonry walls. A concrete footing is required for a wall with a brick or stone veneer. Also, you will need a 1-inch air space between the veneer and the wall it covers.

Artificial stone is also available as a veneer. It is less expensive than real stone and is easier to install because it is lighter in weight and no concrete footing is required.

With real stone, every installation is unique because no two stones are exactly alike. Artificial stones are more uniform in appearance because they are formed of stucco that has been poured into molds and then painted. Although artificial stones have proven to be long lasting, they cannot be considered as permanent as real stone.

New cedar shingle siding and a well-maintained cedar roof and white trim are thoughtfully chosen upgrades that add distinction to this home.

Replacing the Siding

The most common choices of siding, listed in order by their cost-effectiveness based on their lasting quality, are wood plank siding, plywood siding, stucco, pressed-wood siding, and vinyl siding.

Wood plank siding is second in lasting quality only to brick and stone, and for this reason it is the most cost-effective exterior wallcovering. It can be applied vertically, horizontally, or diagonally. If the house is currently sided with wood planks, every effort should be made to restore what exists. Properly maintained, wood plank siding should never have to be replaced—only refinished.

Plywood siding is far superior to vinyl, stucco, and pressed-wood siding but is not as good as wood plank siding. Proper maintenance is required to prevent delamination. If plywood siding is the replacement material of choice, and your budget allows, it should be made from redwood or cedar. Fir siding will not last nearly as long. (If wood shingles are the material of choice, they should be applied over a solid siding, such as plywood, with a layer of felt paper between the shingles and the solid siding.)

Stucco is very brittle, and in areas where houses shift, it has a tendency to crack. To repair cracked stucco, see page 20.

Pressed-hardboard plank or sheet siding is less apt to crack than stucco, but it expands and contracts radically compared to real wood. This movement can result in permanent buckling, especially with materials less than a ½ inch thick. When this material is used on the exterior of a house, it should be thoroughly painted, since moisture will damage pressed-wood siding more quickly than any other siding material.

Vinyl siding is preferred by some but has some drawbacks because it cannot be painted, it oxidizes, it has no insulative value, and it is easily damaged and costly to repair. In addition, vinyl trim is generally flimsy.

The best re-siding job includes removal of the old surface, but this is expensive and not absolutely necessary. If you choose to add a second layer, you should be aware of a few minor drawbacks.

First, if the existing surface is irregular, you will have to smooth it by using furring strips to prevent the irregularities from showing. Second, you will have to use thicker window and door trim to compensate for the increased wall thickness. Third, you will have to extend electrical outlets, light boxes, and water faucets. In addition, if the existing siding is wood, all areas with fungus or structural pest damage should be repaired.

Adding Slope to a Flat Roof

In a neighborhood of houses with sloped roofs, a flat-roofed house can be perceived as having less value. Adding slope to a flat roof can be cost-efficient if you want to get the best return when selling a house in such a neighborhood.

When adding slope to a roof, get help from an engineer. A sloped roof may redistribute weight, adding load to different parts of the house. A qualified engineer can determine whether this is the case and compensate for it. The roof must be properly designed to hold the type of roofing material that will be used. A stronger frame is needed to hold a tile roof than one covered with composition shingles. This determination can also be made by the structural engineer.

The old roofing material should be completely removed to take weight off the structure. Use this opportunity to inspect for fungus damage. Some costs to consider when adding a slope roof include those of adding insulation and extending chimneys, plumbing vent pipes, exhaust vent pipes, and skylight wells. (This is an opportune time to add more skylights.) You may also have to alter incoming utility wires (telephone, television cable, and electric wires).

Adding a Dormer

You can add a dormer to create additional floor space in the attic-level living quarters or simply to add a window through the sloped surface of the roof. Builders often add false dormers for aesthetic appeal, making the roof more interesting to look at and giving the house the appearance of being larger.

The most logical times to build a dormer are when the existing roof cover is nearly

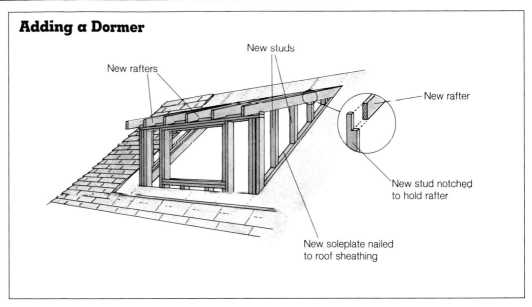

Adding a Dormer

New studs

New rafters

New rafter

New stud notched to hold rafter

New soleplate nailed to roof sheathing

new, just prior to having roof care performed, or just prior to adding a new roof. This is because the area of roof adjacent to the dormer will receive a lot of wear during construction, which may damage older and more brittle roof coverings. New roof coverings are more pliable and not as susceptible to damage.

A false dormer can be added to most roofs without major structural changes. However, even a false dormer can cost several thousand dollars to build. Although the inside of a false dormer can be finished off with window dressings such as drapes or blinds, most people paint the inside of the window with black paint.

Dormers can also be used to create extravagant skylights. However, this is best done only in more expensive neighborhoods where selling prices might support the high cost of such a project.

Planning a Complete Face-Lift

Older homes with deteriorated or outdated fronts can be revitalized very cost-effectively. Paint and newly fashioned decorative trim should be the first consideration, but if you don't think they will be sufficient, new exterior siding is the next logical choice. It may allow the addition of shutters, planter boxes, or an interesting trim color scheme that wouldn't have been possible with the old siding.

Curb appeal is dictated primarily by the appearance of the front of a house, so when you have to make changes that may negatively affect the exterior, make them at the sides and the rear of the house if possible, not the front. If you are considering a face-lift to the entire front of the house, contact a designer or an architect, who will provide a drawing (perhaps in perspective) to show you what the new front will look like after the work is done.

A complete face-lift can also include the addition of a porch with a sloped roof, a new front door, or a bay window. This is an excellent time to replace windows most cost-effectively.

Installing a Spa or Swimming Pool

Not every home improvement is as cost-effective as it is enjoyable. Although a spa is a slightly better investment than a swimming pool, both these features are among the least cost-effective of all home improvements, according to national surveys. Barely 20 percent return can be expected on these investments in general. Yet in a neighborhood where many pools exist, they are considered a valuable feature.

This is not to say that you shouldn't purchase a spa or build a pool, if having one is important to you. It is a matter of personal choice, not potential monetary gain.

THE KITCHEN

A cost-effective kitchen improvement can be as simple as adding a soap dispenser or as dramatic as installing new cabinets and countertops. The kitchen offers more possibilities for alteration than any other room in the house. In fact, nearly every interior improvement suggested in this book can be implemented in the kitchen—even some improvements you might not think of specifically for this room. For example, a garden window is a good place to display decorative cooking utensils. A skylight can create a sunny breakfast nook and brighten a dark work space. And a fireplace provides a place for indoor barbecuing as well as adding warmth and charm.

Because the kitchen is the primary work center of most homes, when a renovation is being planned, all the features of the room should be carefully considered—lighting, traffic flow, distance between work stations (sink, refrigerator, and range), counter space, storage, ventilation, and safety. Carefully balancing these features is what makes the kitchen functional.

Skylights, a sloped roof, hardwood floors, and white cabinets have made a small galley kitchen into a delightful work space. The cabinet doors beside the sink countertop conceal appliances, the refrigerator is faced with white painted doors, and a small laundry area is borrowed from the end of a long hallway.

SMALL KITCHEN UPGRADES

Without spending a lot of money, a do–it–yourselfer can complete any of several small upgrades that will make the kitchen better looking, more convenient, and safer. These small projects cost less than $500 and can be completed in one to two days.

Repairing a Faucet

To enhance the value of an otherwise good-looking sink area, it is important to have a properly maintained faucet. If there is residue where the shine used to be, a faulty gasket or washer is probably to blame. It has let water leak onto polished metal parts, where the water has evaporated and left mineral salt residue.

A faulty gasket or washer is best repaired immediately, since a proper fix becomes more complicated when the condition is allowed to continue for an extended period of time. Mineral deposits build up, making disassembly more difficult.

Use a 10 percent solution of sodium carbonate to dissolve the alkaline buildup before attempting a repair. You can purchase this raw chemical in small quantities from a photography shop, pharmacy, or laboratory supply company.

Almost everyone is familiar with the gaskets in the faucet valve, but another gasket that is likely to cause problems is the O-ring located at the swivel point of the spout. If the faucet is leaking at this junction, remove the spout; the O-ring is at its base. To fix the leak, clean off the corrosion and alkaline buildup, and then replace the ring with a new one.

Replacing a Faucet

The faucet is the most-used device in the kitchen, so when choosing a replacement, the prime considerations should be personal preference and convenience, ease of repair, quality of the mechanism, and the exterior finish.

Faucets that are made of solid brass (not brass-plated metal) and that have been machined to close tolerances operate more smoothly and are less likely to leak than lesser-quality faucets. Smooth operation means better control of water flow.

Well-made faucets (those that will last 10 years or more) will most likely come from the best-known manufacturers of plumbing fixtures. Inexpensive faucets may look good, but the low-end models are usually constructed at least in part of plastic. Although certain plastic parts are acceptable, plastic housings coated with silver paint simply don't hold up for very long.

The single-lever faucet has replaced the two-handle type in popularity for two reasons: It provides for quick, easy, one-handed control of both water flow and temperature, and fewer moving parts make even the most expensive faucet easy and inexpensive to repair. Modern single-lever faucets use modular valve and gasket kits that are almost as easy to replace as a battery in a flashlight.

Adding a Vegetable Spray or Soap Dispenser

Although a prospective buyer may not notice a fancy faucet, accessories always get a second glance. An extra 10 percent added to the price of a kitchen faucet will cover the cost of a vegetable spray attachment.

Another inexpensive feature that can improve convenience is an in-sink soap dispenser. They are easy to install, easy to refill (the pump lifts out, exposing the fill hole), and require no maintenance. Repairing one is as simple as lifting out the pump and replacing it with a new one.

You can purchase and install a soap dispenser separately from a faucet. If the sink doesn't have a spare hole, you can drill one with a ¾-inch carbide-tipped bit. Even a porcelain-coated cast-iron sink can be drilled, although care should be taken not to damage the porcelain finish. When drilling porcelain, you must cool the area with water. To do this, create a water reservoir by damming the surrounding area with modeling clay.

Upgrading a Sink

Before replacing a sink, try cleaning it. For a porcelain sink, make a paste of pumice powder mixed with turpentine. Wipe it onto the surface of the sink with a rag, and then polish it with a buffing pad on an electric drill. This simple procedure will remove rust and other stains and bring a new shine to even the most heavily pitted surface. Use a clean buffing pad and car wax to add a final glow. Car wax also works wonders on chrome accessories.

Caution: Pumice will damage stainless steel and other nonporcelain finishes.

It's time to refinish a kitchen sink when a replacement is too costly, when cleaning isn't effective, or when the color needs to be changed. But refinishing is not always the best alternative. If the cost of purchasing and installing a new sink is the same as or even slightly more than the cost of refinishing, it is more cost-effective to replace the sink rather than refinish it.

You can add five years or more to the life of practically any sink by refinishing it. In this process a special paint is applied and then, in most instances, heat-cured. Since the paint comes in a variety of colors, you can change an outdated color during this process. Refinishing is not permanent, but it can defer the cost of replacement for many years. Look in the yellow pages under Plumbing Fixtures—Refinishing to find someone to do this for you. It is wise to hire a company that offers at least a five-year guarantee.

Kitchen Upgrades

For an overview of the kitchen, before and after remodeling, see pages 6 and 7.

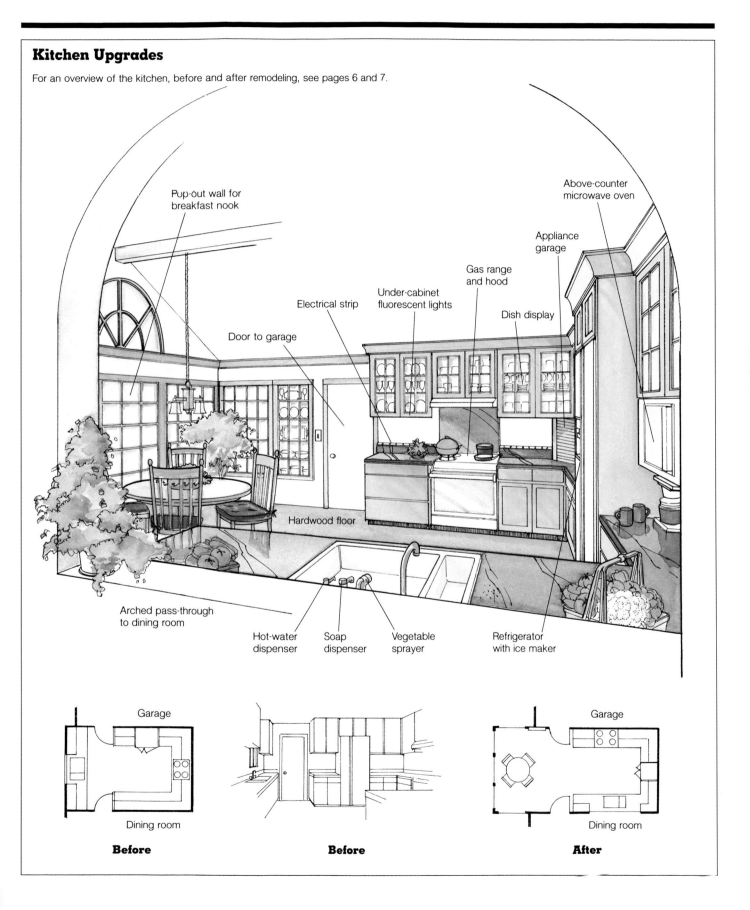

Pop-out wall for breakfast nook

Above-counter microwave oven

Appliance garage

Gas range and hood

Under-cabinet fluorescent lights

Electrical strip

Dish display

Door to garage

Hardwood floor

Arched pass-through to dining room

Hot-water dispenser

Soap dispenser

Vegetable sprayer

Refrigerator with ice maker

Garage

Dining room

Before

Before

Garage

Dining room

After

Replacing a Sink

There are no special rules for choosing between sinks having one or two compartments. It depends solely on space limitations and personal taste. Sinks with one compartment are available in the smallest sizes; hence they are more practical for small, compact kitchens. Choose a sink appropriate to the size of the kitchen; a sink that is too large can overwhelm a small space and make it look even smaller and less efficient.

Sink replacement is affected by the existing countertop. The sink rim (outermost edge) must be compatible with the countertop into which it will be installed. There are two different basic rim styles—tile recessed and self-rimming.

Tile-Recessed Rim Style

A tile-recessed rim is designed to be placed into countertops made of ceramic, porcelain, marble, or granite tile. The key is not the surface material itself but the position of the installed sink—the sink is recessed below the finished surface of the tile, its edge is encased in mortar, and then it is trimmed from above. With this type of rim, the top edge of the sink is almost an inch below the surface of the surrounding counter, making counter cleaning easy compared to other types of installations.

A high-quality recessed sink installation includes a tiled surface that slopes gently (with a slope not readily visible) toward the sink, so that water will not stand on the countertop.

The hidden rim of the tile-recessed sink incorporates an upturned lip that sheds water toward the sink compartment, helping to prevent water from traveling beyond the tile-sink connection into the cabinetry. Laying a sink that does not have a proper rim into tile can be costly, since this would increase the chance of damage to the undercounter support surface and other adjacent wood parts. Because most of these surfaces are hidden from view, damage usually becomes a serious problem long before it is discovered.

A new type of recessed sink suitable for tile countertops is the surface-mounted style. With this style, the top surface of the rim of the sink is placed flush with the top surface of the countertop tiles. This type of sink, like its recessed-mounted counterpart, is not recommended for use with plastic laminate countertops, because it is difficult to create an adequate water seal.

A drawback to the surface-mounted rim is that it derives most of its ability to shed water from the grout connection between the tile and the sink. Even the slightest house movement will cause grout to crack. Take the cost of special maintenance (regular regrouting) into consideration before selecting this model in areas where ground movement or house shifting are commonplace.

Self-Rimming Style

The self-rimming cast-iron type of sink, in which the sink rises into a rim that rests above the level of the countertop, is by far the most popular, even though mopping up a flooded countertop can be slightly more difficult with this style, and the cost

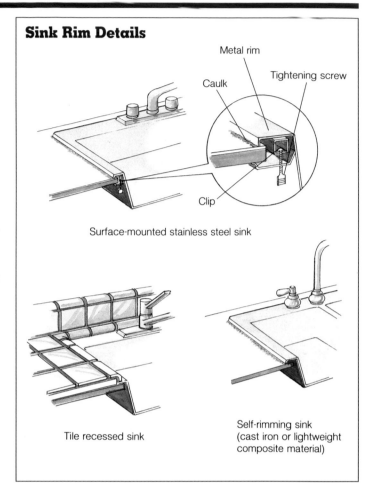

Sink Rim Details

Metal rim

Caulk

Tightening screw

Clip

Surface-mounted stainless steel sink

Tile recessed sink

Self-rimming sink (cast iron or lightweight composite material)

of tile-recessed and self-rimming sinks are within pennies of each other. Self-rimming sinks are easier to install (resulting in less overall cost) and can be used in conjunction with any type of countertop.

The installation process is easy. Cut an opening into the countertop (a template for this purpose is provided with the sink). Caulk the underside of the rim and drop the sink into place. Then touch up by adding another bead of silicone caulk between the sink rim and the countertop. No tile contractor is needed, and the only chance for a leak is if the visible bead of caulk is not maintained. Recaulk a self-rimming sink at least once a year. That may seem excessive, but it will prevent one of the leading causes of moisture damage in the house.

Finishes and Compartment Configurations

The sink should fit comfortably into the counter configuration. Given ample counter space, a multicompartment sink is convenient and is impressive to prospective home buyers. Sink depth is another consideration. The deeper the sink the more versatile—and expensive—it is.

Stainless steel sinks are attractive when new but scratch easily and require special cleaning compounds to maintain the original shine. If you are considering stainless steel, it is wise to remember that the gauge (thickness) of the metal has a great deal to do with its lasting quality. Most stainless steel sinks are available in three thicknesses: 20, 18, and 16 gauge. Although the latter is the thickest and the most resistant to dents and bending, it is designed primarily for commercial use and isn't available in a wide range of styles, so 18 gauge is the next best choice.

Porcelain is an extremely popular sink finish; it has a high gloss and comes in a myriad of colors. Porcelain is generally applied to either a pressed steel or molded cast-iron shell, with pressed steel being less expensive and more prone to chipping. Cast iron is the better base. It is quieter when the disposer is running, it keeps water warmer longer, and it is stronger and longer lasting than pressed steel.

Chips can be repaired in any porcelain sink regardless of the base materials. Avoid the do-it-yourself, paint-on type of patch kit; the repairs seldom look professional and can detract from the value of the sink almost as much as the chip. Professional sink-repair companies can make an almost invisible patch in a porcelain sink for about a third of the cost to replace the sink.

Lightweight composite materials are a recent development in sink finishes. They are almost as thin as stainless steel and come in a variety of designer colors. Sinks made of acrylic and fiberglass are also available but are not in wide use. Some homeowners may be willing to test the lasting quality of these products, but it is safer to stay with time-proven

materials, such as stainless steel and cast iron.

How to Replace a Tile-Recessed Sink

Several methods are available for replacing an old-fashioned sink surrounded by tile. Although you can use another tile-recessed sink, the least expensive alternative is to use a self-rimming sink for the replacement. Interestingly, many self-rimming sinks have the same inside dimensions as their tile-recessed counterparts, but the rim portion is wider. This makes covering the hole created by the removal of a tile-recessed sink easy to hide. In addition, you can install a larger self-rimming sink by carefully cutting back the existing tile counter with a masonry blade mounted in a small circular power saw.

Replacing a tile-recessed sink with another of the same style, especially when the surrounding existing tile is irreplaceable, can be very expensive. Some companies hand-paint tile to any specification. A local ceramic tile distributor can usually help you find such a craftsperson.

It is less expensive to purchase new ceramic tile sink trim in a contrasting or complementary color. Make your selection carefully. A bad color match can detract from the overall appearance.

Regardless of the type of sink you use for the replacement, success will depend on the painstakingly slow and careful removal of the existing sink trim tiles. Expect to damage the trim tile during removal. It is more important to prevent damage to the adjacent

field tiles. Most tile-recessed sinks can be removed easily once the sink trim tiles are out of the way.

Cleaning Grout and Tile

The white powder that builds up on grout is mineral salt efflorescence. Most apparent on medium- and dark-colored grout, it is best removed with white vinegar. Remove stains from light-colored grout with a strong solution of liquid household bleach applied vigorously with a stiff nylon brush.

Caution: Never mix bleach with ammonia or cleansers containing ammonia. The combination is lethal and can create a poisonous vapor similar to mustard gas.

Ceramic tile can be cleaned with any one of several nonabrasive, off-the-shelf cleaning products. For more information on these products, see the list of associations on page 108 for the addresses of the Ceramic Tile Institute and the Tile Council of America.

Cleaning Plastic Laminate Surfaces and Linoleum

Laminates are not affected by most petrochemical agents. An old carpenter's trick is to use lacquer thinner to remove especially tough scuff marks on plastic laminate countertops and linoleum. Use lacquer thinner sparingly on linoleum. Test a hidden area first to ensure that the chemical will not damage the surface. Good ventilation is an absolute must when you are using lacquer thinner indoors. The vapors are toxic

and highly flammable. Anyone with respiratory problems should not be present during the cleaning process. Wear gloves and eye protection.

Cleaning Porcelain and Fiberglass

Turpentine is effective for cleaning porcelain and fiberglass surfaces, but adding salt to create a paste is even better. Not many stains get by this combination. Turpentine is a petrochemical by-product and should be used with gloves and eye protection in a well-ventilated area.

Cleaning Wood Butcher-Block Countertops

Clean butcher block with a mild solution of liquid dish soap and water scrubbed in with a nylon brush or scrubbing pad. After the surface has dried thoroughly, apply a coat of mineral oil or vegetable oil. If the wood grain raises during the washing process, use sandpaper to smooth the surface before applying the oil. Do not use steel wool or wet-and-dry sandpaper on butcher block. These materials release fibers and grains that might become embedded in the wood.

Cleaning Fine Wood Cabinets (and Furniture)

A mixture of linseed oil, turpentine, and water is an effective cleaner for fine wood furniture and cabinetry. Mix 3 tablespoons of turpentine together with 3 tablespoons of linseed oil, and then blend this into 1 quart of boiling water. Wearing rubber gloves, dip a rag into the cleaner and wring it out until barely damp. Wash small areas at a time (2 to 3 square feet), and then dry immediately with a clean, soft cloth. When the mixture cools it will separate. Don't reuse the solution; discard it and make another batch.

Cleaning Glass, Appliances, and Porcelain

One quarter cup of rubbing alcohol mixed with a quart of water cleans appliances, glass, and highly polished porcelain tile. The alcohol leaves no streaks, and it disinfects as well.

Eradicating Mildew

Use the following mixture to eradicate mildew: ⅓ cup of powdered laundry detergent and 1 quart of liquid laundry bleach mixed with 3 quarts of warm water. Add the bleach to the water and then mix in the laundry detergent. Even though the solution is fairly mild, wear rubber gloves and eye protection. Keep the surface wet until the bleach turns the gray-black mildew white. Rinse thoroughly with water. This solution is safe for most surfaces, including painted walls, and can be used indoors or outdoors.

Caution: Never mix bleach with ammonia or cleansers containing ammonia; the combination produces a lethal gas.

Adding a Dimmer Switch

Easy and inexpensive to install, the dimmer switch (rheostat) seems to have more impact on the average consumer than projects costing hundreds of dollars.

Dimmer switches are available in a wide range of styles and prices; the lower-priced models work just as well as the expensive ones. They all do the same thing: control the intensity of illumination at the light fixture. For example, the over-the-sink fixture is often a single-bulb incandescent light operated by an independent switch. Leaving that light on during the meal at 25 percent of normal intensity wouldn't be too bright to distract from the meal and would provide sufficient lighting to make trips to the kitchen safe.

Dimmer switches are available in three types: the rotating control (like the volume knob on a radio), the toggle (like a regular light switch), and the slide switch (with a separate on-off button). The cost is about the same, but the toggle and slide switches have a cleaner look and operate more quietly than some of the rotating controls, which have a tendency to hum.

Even the most expensive dimmer switches can be noisy. Make sure that the switch being purchased has a money-back guarantee in case it hums when in operation. Asking after the fact may not guarantee a refund.

A more significant difference among dimmer switches is whether they are two-way (single-pole) or three-way. Use a two-way dimmer where

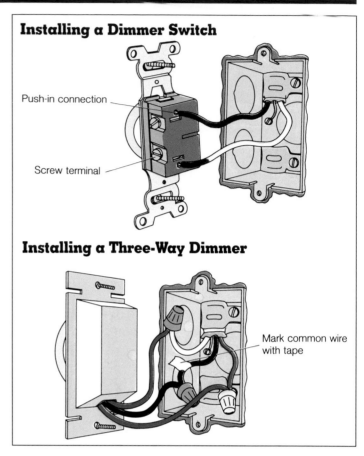

Installing a Dimmer Switch

Push-in connection

Screw terminal

Installing a Three-Way Dimmer

Mark common wire with tape

only one switch controls the light(s). A three-way dimmer must be used to replace a switch when two switches control the light(s).

Dimmers cannot be used with conventional fluorescent lights. You can, however, install special ballasts that allow you to use a fluorescent light with a dimmer.

Caution: Before attempting an electrical project, it is important to be absolutely sure that the power is turned off—preferably at the breaker panel.

Upgrading a Light Fixture

A tarnished or worn light fixture can detract from the overall appearance of a room. Refinishing a light fixture

rather than replacing it is one of the most cost-effective home improvements, especially if the fixture is 50 or more years old.

The older the fixture the better the chance that it is made of solid brass or pewter (or a combination of the two). Whereas most of today's manufacturers would never consider painting solid brass or pewter, in bygone days the practice was commonplace. To find out whether a fixture is solid brass instead of brass plate, scratch a hidden surface with a nail or a screwdriver. Solid brass will yield a brass-colored scratch. If the fixture is brass plate, the best bet is to consider painting it. Replating is not cost-effective.

Fixtures made of cast iron or steel are almost impossible to damage during the paint stripping and cleaning process and are the easiest to paint.

Most brass or pewter light fixtures can be brought to like-new condition in an afternoon with paint remover, very fine steel wool, and brass polish. In cases where pitting has occurred, you can bring both brass and pewter back to life by sanding before polishing.

For best results, dismantle elaborate fixtures before refinishing, and then rewire them during reassembly. For hidden wiring, use 16-gauge stranded copper wire in a THHN casing. If decorative wiring is required, be sure to use a UL-approved material in a gauge that will support the total wattage of the bulbs.

Polish refinished brass, and then apply a corrosion inhibitor. Several spray-on products are available for this purpose. A coat of clear lacquer is one possibility, but it is difficult to remove when the fixture begins to tarnish. Unprotected brass will begin to tarnish immediately.

Although replacing a light fixture is easier than refinishing it, replacement is more costly. The price of light fixtures includes a high markup, so that lights are expensive even with the 20 to 30 percent discount that you can expect in a lighting store. (It is not uncommon for contractors to purchase light fixtures at a discount of "50 and 10," that is, 50 percent off retail and 10 percent off the remaining 50 percent, or 55 percent off retail.)

When replacing a light fixture, it is important to keep quality as well as appearance in mind. Good-quality fixtures are made of solid metal (brass is best) and have glass instead of plastic shades. Crystal is an alternative to glass because of the interesting way that it refracts light. Avoid using an intricate light fixture in the kitchen. Cleaning and maintenance can be a real chore in a room that generates so much greasy steam. Clean lines make for easy-to-clean surfaces.

Replacing Incandescent With Fluorescent Lighting

The least expensive of all lighting improvements consists of replacing a regular incandescent bulb with a fluorescent tube. The room will brighten and the electric bill will decrease. In addition, fluorescent lighting will reduce the load on old wiring, making the house safer.

Many building agencies actually require that fluorescent lighting be at least 50 percent of the lighting used in the kitchen and bath in both new and remodeled homes. The reason: maximum light and energy efficiency.

Adding Task Lighting

Task lighting is the term given to light fixtures installed in specific locations where activities can be accomplished more comfortably with the aid of an additional source of illumination.

Although task lighting in the kitchen isn't a new concept, it is more affordable than ever before.

The most common type is the under-cabinet fixture (mounted on the bottom of the upper cabinets). Other task lighting includes recessed or surface-mounted ceiling fixtures, hanging fixtures, or a combination of these.

Be careful when adding new lights to an existing electrical line, especially in homes with older electrical circuits already taxed by numerous appliances. It is a common misconception that adding a 75-watt light bulb will have less effect on an existing electrical circuit than a small appliance of greater wattage. In fact, small appliances

are generally used for short periods of time, whereas lights often remain on for several hours at a time.

The most cost-efficient way to add any type of task lighting to the kitchen is to install all the lights at one time. This is because when you add a new light fixture you should also add a new circuit at the electric panel. This can double the cost of adding just one light with a switch. The good news is that one electrical circuit for lighting will handle several light fixtures.

Adding Low-Voltage Lighting

Low-voltage light fixtures have an advantage over the conventional type in that they place

Fluorescent fixtures were installed under the upper cabinets to illuminate the countertop and highlight the handsome tilework in this remodeled kitchen.

Adding Kitchen Accessories

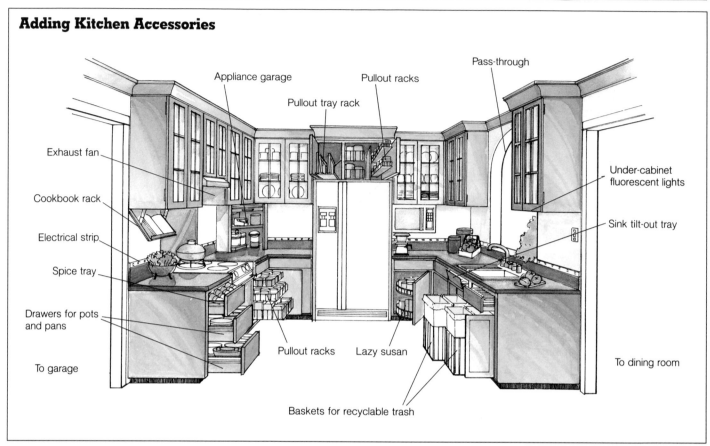

Exhaust fan
Cookbook rack
Electrical strip
Spice tray
Drawers for pots and pans
To garage
Appliance garage
Pullout tray rack
Pullout racks
Pass-through
Under-cabinet fluorescent lights
Sink tilt-out tray
To dining room
Pullout racks
Lazy susan
Baskets for recyclable trash

less stress on existing electrical circuits; however, they are usually more expensive. In addition, high-intensity, low-voltage light bulbs are among the most expensive bulbs, they burn out faster than other bulbs, and they may fluctuate in intensity during operation (a condition called strobing).

When considering low-voltage interior lighting, it is important to see a live demonstration in a room with all the other lights turned off. Shine the low-voltage light onto a wall that you can view from several angles. Give the eye time to adjust to the brightness before moving from position to position. Some angles will not reveal the effect as readily as others. Dimming the lights usually increases the strobing effect.

Installing a GFCI Device

The National Electrical Code now requires ground fault circuit interrupters (GFCI) at some electrical outlets located in the kitchen. Most building agencies enforce this rule on electrical outlets that are located within 6 feet of a sink. GFCI circuit breakers are safer than normal circuits because they break much faster and because they detect overload on both positive and neutral lines. Regular fusing detects overload only on the positive line. This improvement probably will not bring any return on investment, but it will certainly make the kitchen safer. You can install a GFCI receptacle into an existing plug outlet box in about 20 minutes.

Adding Cabinet Accessories

Installing ready-made plastic or wire pullouts solves the problem of how to reach the back of the shelf in lower cabinets. Each of these lightweight sliding trays is capable of holding a half-dozen or more heavy frying pans. It is wise to select pullouts in a width narrower than the door behind which they will be installed, so that you won't have to open two doors to get to one pullout. If you aren't handy with tools or you want the choice of a full line of these options, contact a local cabinetmaker. They have access to hundreds of cabinet accessories that can't be found in home-improvement centers.

Cabinets with false drawer fronts below the cooktop or sink can be fitted with a tilt-out that can add storage space and versatility. Tilt-outs can be used to store spices, scouring pads, and other small items in the otherwise unused space between the front of the cabinet and the sink or cooktop. Although tilt-outs are not as easy to install as pullouts, the project can be completed in an afternoon. For each tilt-out you will need two hinges, which should match those on the existing cabinets. You will also need a tilt-out tray, which you can purchase or make from a scrap of wood.

Kits for appliance garages are available through all major cabinet-supply distributors. You can assemble, stain and varnish (or paint), and install an appliance garage in a weekend. Appliance garages are most versatile when a plug is available within, but even without one they are worth the investment for the tidy look and clean lines they lend to the countertop.

For a home with toddlers, it is wise to consider child-proofing doors and drawers with safety latches. Hidden latches are the most convenient to use and easiest to install, but the best protection is the more expensive key lock. It can be installed in a wood cabinet door in less than an hour. A double door configuration takes a little longer and requires the addition of a latch mounted on the inside of the second door.

Adding a Small Cabinet

You can use empty wall space in a kitchen for extra storage. A 2- or 3-foot-long cabinet costs less than a good cast-iron sink. Like furniture and light fixtures, modular cabinets usually have a considerable markup. A wise shopper can save 30 to 70 percent off the retail price of most brands.

When shopping for a ready-made base cabinet, try to find one in a size, color, and style to match the existing cabinets. When the new cabinet is not immediately adjacent to existing ones, casework detail and color can vary slightly without detracting from appearance. In such an installation the countertop can be made of a different material and actually add interest to the room.

First, find a cabinet of the right length. Most kitchen base cabinets are 24 inches deep; you can shorten this dimension if necessary with a handsaw, nails, and glue. Keep in mind that if the cabinet has drawers, you must also shorten the drawers and the tracks on which they slide—a more difficult alteration.

After finding the right size cabinet, consider doors and drawer fronts. You can purchase these individually from a local cabinetmaker. Buying all new doors and then staining or painting them can be far less expensive than having the entire cabinet custom-made.

Adding a base cabinet to an existing run, rather than as a separate installation, can be expensive—old and new must match precisely, and lengthening a countertop can, in some cases, require a full replacement. Remember, the kitchen is an important room in calculating resale value and will not be enhanced by mismatched styles.

Because a wall cabinet does not require a countertop or drawers, the job of adding one is less complicated than that of adding a base cabinet. However, not every manufacturer makes wall cabinets that will align with the bottoms of existing cabinets and be tall enough to reach an 8-foot ceiling. Be careful not to vary in style here. If you can't find a good match, consider a custom-made cabinet.

The trick to installing a wall cabinet is to make sure that there is a positive connection with existing wall studs. Do not use expansion screws or toggle bolts. Instead, hold the new cabinet in place with temporary

supports, then predrill the wall studs and the mounting strip at the top and/or bottom ends of the cabinet. Use 3- or 3½-inch-long wallboard screws for the connection. Two screws per linear foot of cabinet width (one at the top and one at the bottom) will be sufficient.

Painting Cabinets

Painting your kitchen cabinets can give your kitchen a fresh, new look unmatched by any other project in the same cost range.

As is the case with any painting project, the best results are achieved by careful preparation. Do not remove old paint completely. If several coats exist, remove only the top three or four. Attempting to remove all the paint down to the wood will cause unnecessary work and expense, and you could damage the cabinets themselves in the process.

Fill all voids, dents, scratches, and nicks before sanding the cabinets. It is wise to begin with a medium sandpaper (80 grit), and then proceed to fine (150 grit) and finally extrafine (400 grit). If the wood feels like glass after it has been sanded, it will look like glass when painted.

The prime coat creates a bond between the existing finish and the new layer of paint, lightens a dark surface, and seals and fills the sanded

The need for plentiful storage led to a handsome addition to this galley kitchen, with an inviting window seat in the eating area.

surface. Do not apply the primer so thickly that it covers the old finish completely unless you are lightening dark cabinets. The primer should be similar in color but not identical to the finish coat, so that you can see any spots you've missed when painting. Sand the primed surface with 400- to 600-grit sandpaper. Be careful not to sand through to the wood. If this happens, reprime and touch-sand the area.

A careful painter can easily avoid the three most common mistakes when applying the finish coat: working in a dusty area, failing to use clean paint and painting equipment, and trying to do the job in one coat.

First, make sure that the work area is well ventilated, and then completely clean and vacuum the room and area adjacent to where the cabinets will be painted. Next, wipe the cabinets with a dust-free cloth dipped in the proper solvent (use a sparing amount). Then, use cheesecloth or a store-bought paint strainer to filter the paint. Unfiltered paint and dusty surroundings will result in a rough finished surface no matter how well the cabinets were stripped and sanded.

If the paint is too thick or is applied too heavily, it will run before it flows to a smooth finish. Thin oil-based paint to a watery consistency for the first of two finish coats. (Use 20 percent solvent and 80 percent paint.) Filter the paint after thinning it. Once applied, the wet coat should be transparent; you should be able to see the primer. Let the first coat dry, then sand lightly and apply a second finish coat.

Varnishing Cabinets

Bringing new life to stained and varnished cabinets is much easier than repainting painted cabinets. Again, success lies in professional preparation and in knowing what to expect during the process.

First, wash the cabinets with TSP. This removes grease and other residue from the surface and slightly etches the existing finish. Next, lightly sand all surfaces with 400- to 600-grit wet-and-dry sandpaper. Keep the sandpaper wet with water at all times. The sanding process will turn the varnished surface a milky white, and as it dries it will have a matte and lightly scratched appearance. This is normal. Sanding too much could damage the stained surface beneath the varnish. Finally, vacuum the work area thoroughly, wipe all surfaces with paint thinner or lacquer thinner on a soft, lint-free cloth, and then apply the first coat of finish. It is important to have good ventilation when working with chemicals that generate flammable and toxic vapors.

To make the cabinets look new again, apply two to four coats of clear varnish or a similar product. Lightly sand between coats with water and 600-grit wet-and-dry sandpaper. Make sure that the coat to be sanded is completely dry. It is wise to wait twice as long as the instructions on the can recommend. Varnish takes longer to dry in cool temperatures or high humidity.

Applying Wallcoverings

When selecting a wallcovering for the kitchen, keep in mind the same considerations concerning color and pattern that apply to the selection of paint—essentially, low-key patterns are more appealing to a wider range of tastes.

Wall preparation is as important when you are putting up a wallcovering as when

you are painting. Wall surfaces should be thoroughly cleaned, smoothed with a filler (such as joint compound) if necessary, and then primed with oil-based paint. Although you can apply a plain white base layer of wallpaper to rough wall surfaces to smooth them, smoothing the wall itself is the way professional paperhangers do it. Priming with oil-based paint will prevent the adhesive from penetrating too deeply into the

This kitchen upgrade features the original cabinets with new chrome drawer pulls to match the chrome faucet and light fixture over the sink.

surface of the plaster or wallboard, which will allow for easy removal later. Ease of removal can be a big selling feature to a prospective buyer who prefers paint or another wallcovering pattern.

It is especially important in the kitchen to use a wallcovering that will resist damage from grease and harsh cleaning products. Although some heavier papers hold up well, vinyl-coated ones are best. Note that special adhesives are required when you are applying vinyl-coated wallcoverings. Using the wrong adhesive could allow mildew to grow between the wall surface and the wallpaper. It will show up as black splotches a few days after the paper has been installed.

A tip from the pros: Whether or not the wallcovering is prepasted, apply a coat of paste by hand. Overwetting a prepasted wallcovering can completely remove all the adhesive that was applied at the factory. Thoroughly smoothing the covering to the wall to remove air pockets is also very important. The other secret to a good job is to have plenty of sharp razor blades on hand (30 or more for the average room). A new razor blade will be good for two or three cuts and should then be saved for a later use that doesn't require extreme sharpness.

To remove old wallcovering, you must bring the adhesive that bonds it to the wall to a semiliquid state. Two processes are currently available to accomplish this—steaming and enzyme chemical reduction. Regardless of the process you select, you must perforate the surface of the wallcovering so that the steam or enzymes can reach the old adhesive.

A tool specifically made for this purpose, when rolled over the surface of the wallcovering, creates thousands of holes through which steam or enzymes can pass and begin to dissolve the paste. Rubbing the teeth of a handsaw across the surface of the wallcovering will produce a similar result; however, a zealous hand can damage the surface of the underlying wall, which can be costly to repair. Working from the top down when removing wallcovering allows gravity to help the process along.

Regrouting Ceramic Tile

Usually the first part of a ceramic tile installation to show wear is the grout. Natural settlement of a newly installed counter surface and general house movement are the culprits. Because tile grout is a cement-based material, it is brittle. When the house moves, grout cracks, and the resulting valleys trap food and allow water to pass to the wood below.

When regrouting it is important to match the existing grout color. Tile stores have samples of grout on hand for making a comparison.

First, clean the cracks with bleach and a nylon scrub brush. You can use a hair dryer to remove excess moisture. Next, widen existing cracks. Grout is made of sand and cement, and the cracks must be wide enough for the granules of sand in the new grout to fit. Use an awl, a screwdriver, a chisel, or a sharpened piece of hardwood—$\frac{1}{8}$ to $\frac{1}{4}$ inch in depth is plenty. Remove all the loose grout. The more you remove, the better the chance that the new grout will adhere.

Once you have prepared the surface, mix the grout. An old trick is to omit about 20 percent of the water recommended by the grout manufacturer and replace it with clear-drying white glue. The mucilage helps to bond the new grout to the old and is an excellent sealant as well.

You can use a grout trowel or a flat piece of hard rubber to force the grout mixture into the cracks. Remove excess grout with a slightly dampened paper towel. It is important to clean as much of the grout from the tile surfaces as possible while the grout is still wet. It becomes almost impossible to remove once it dries. To easily remove the light film that will be left on the tile when the job

Thoughtful touches in this remodeled kitchen include a tiled cooking area (above) that is echoed in the tiled back splash in the photo at left.

is completed and everything is dry, use a solution of 10 percent vinegar and 90 percent water.

After about a week (assuming that no white, powdery mineral salts have surfaced; see page 37), you can apply a silicone sealer to further protect the grout. Making the grout more water-resistant will help keep it clean and reduce water infiltration.

In a home with a tendency to shift, the best permanent repair to the grout joint between the countertop and the back splash is done with a colored silicone caulk. Caulk is far more flexible than grout and will expand and contract under conditions where grout will crack.

Recaulking the Sink

Since water can pass through almost invisible separations, it is important to maintain the connection between the sink and countertop, whether the sink is a tile-recessed or self-rimming type. Water damage can occur to hidden cabinet parts if there is a break in this connection. Caulking this seam is inexpensive and takes less than 30 minutes once a year.

First, remove as much of the old silicone caulk as possible by scraping it off with a putty knife (being careful not to scratch the porcelain or tile) or a sharp wood stick. Next, clean the area with a strong solution of bleach and water. Then use a hair dryer to dry the area thoroughly. Finally, brush away the last pieces of loose debris, and apply the new layer of caulk.

Repairing a Plastic Laminate Surface

To repair a delaminated plastic laminate surface, you apply heat. First, lay a towel on the damaged area to act as a buffer between the plastic laminate and the heat source. Then use a clothes iron, set on high, to bring the surface up to temperature. The heat of the iron will soften the laminate and the adhesive that binds the surface to the substrate. Once the laminate is hot to the touch, remove the iron and rub the towel with a hard downward pressure over the heated surface until it cools. The new bond will be stronger than the original connection. This process can be used on most plastic laminate surfaces, including cabinets.

Another way to repair a damaged laminate countertop is to cut out and replace the damaged portion. You can install a wood cutting board into a plastic laminate countertop in place of a badly damaged section of the surface. First, purchase a sink rim in a size that is slightly larger than the damaged area (many sizes are available). Next, cut a ¾-inch-thick cutting board to fit the sink rim. Then cut the counter to accept the sink rim, and finally mount the cutting board and the sink rim into the countertop with silicone and the retainer clips that come with the sink rim. The inlaid cutting board makes food preparation easier and solves the damage problem. This is a project to consider even if the countertop isn't damaged.

Adding a Pass-Through Screen

If a sliding window is located between your kitchen and backyard, you can make the two areas more accessible to each other by adding a pass-through screen assembly. This project can improve logistics during garden parties and other backyard activities and will keep out flying pests while letting in fresh air. This little-known option is available from many window companies. It is nothing more than an aluminum track, made to match the frame of an existing window, that holds a sliding screen (similar to a sliding patio door). Installation takes less than 15 minutes.

Refinishing Appliances

When done in conjunction with appliance replacement, appliance refinishing is cost-effective. Repainting all the appliances in a kitchen could be costly, especially if some of them are coming to an end of their useful life. For example, if you are going to replace two or three major appliances you can refinish the remaining few to match. This can help to maintain a good-looking kitchen while stretching the lives of the remaining appliances until you are ready to upgrade them.

Like plumbing-fixture refinishing, appliance painting is not for everyone. In some cases, the painting process can be almost as expensive as the appliance itself; for example, a range hood can usually be replaced for less than the cost of refinishing. This is not true for a late-model refrigerator or oven, however.

You can repaint appliances yourself at home, but for lasting quality the proper paint materials and application process must be used. Appliance paints are made for use on metal, and the paint should be heat-cured (dried).

Adding, Moving, or Replacing Appliances

The biggest consideration when adding or replacing any electrical appliance is its power source. Taxing old electrical circuits with modern appliances, which may use more power, is dangerous. Even if a new appliance is more energy efficient than the one it replaces, it may require an upgraded electrical circuit. When considering an appliance upgrade, it is important to contact an electrical contractor for advice on circuit upgrades and costs. Do this before purchasing or installing any new electrical appliance anywhere in the home, especially the kitchen.

Electrical outlet receptacles for large appliances incorporate a plug face that is designed for a specific combination of voltage and amperage. When replacing the old receptacle with a new one designed to fit the plug on a new appliance, keep in mind that the receptacle must match the size of the wire in the circuit as well as the size of the fuse. Hence, changing the receptacle may also require new wiring and fuses.

It is not uncommon to see built-in dishwashers plugged into the circuit originally dedicated to another appliance, such as the garbage disposer, or vice versa. Either practice increases the danger of fire. The following electrical appliances require their own separate circuits: single ovens, double ovens, cooktops, built-in microwave ovens, built-in dishwashers, built-in trash compactors, instant hot-water dispensers, garbage disposers, some range hoods, built-in food warmers, built-in food processors, and some ice-making machines.

Moving the Microwave Oven Off the Counter

Even in the largest kitchens, counter space is a precious commodity, and countertop microwave ovens take up a great deal of space. Although you can install a microwave oven hood in place of an existing range hood to free up counter space, this is wasteful if an existing countertop microwave oven will be discarded in the process. There is another alternative—a microwave shelf, which is designed to place a countertop microwave oven in the range hood cavity, thereby storing the oven in a more convenient and space-efficient way. The shelf also includes the features of a standard range hood—ventilation and lighting.

The main prerequisite for this project is two studs in the wall where the shelf is to be installed. Countertop microwave ovens are heavy, and the accessory shelf must have a sturdy attachment. Minor costs to refabricate the sheet-metal

exhaust duct should also be considered when pricing this project. Consult an electrical contractor concerning electrical connections.

Adding a Trash Compactor

To accomplish a cost-effective installation of a trash compactor, the cabinet where it is to be installed must be approximately 24 inches deep. If it is an island or a peninsula cabinet, make sure that the entire back of the cabinet is perpendicular to the floor, without the interruption of a toe-kick recess. (This recess will prevent proper installation.) In addition, review the information about electrical considerations on page 44. Having to add a new electrical circuit could cost more than the compactor itself.

Compactors are available in three widths: 12, 15, and 18 inches. An opening that matches one of these widths probably already exists in most cabinets. A slightly larger opening can be used but will require trim strips at the sides.

Once you have selected a location, remove the cabinet door, cut out the base of the cabinet with a saw, and remove any drawer hardware and framing. Then slip the compactor into the hole and adjust the legs so that the unit aligns with the face and top of the opening in the cabinet.

Quieting the Dishwasher or the Garbage Disposer

The problem of a noisy dishwasher is easy and inexpensive to solve for a do-it-yourselfer capable of removing and replacing a built-in dishwasher.

First, disconnect the dishwasher and remove it from the cabinets. Next, lightly cover the housing of the dishwasher and the interior walls of the cabinet with spray adhesive (similar to contact cement). Apply a layer of 1-inch-thick duct insulation (also sprayed with adhesive) to the dishwasher housing and the cavity in the cabinets. Then reinstall and reconnect the appliance. It is important not to place the insulation over the ventilation holes that serve to dissipate heat from the appliance.

Making the garbage disposer operate more quietly is just as simple. First, lightly coat the underside of the sink and one side of 1-inch-thick duct insulation with spray adhesive. Next, apply the insulation to

Bullnosed edges, used instead of more costly trim, soften the lines of the arched pass-through, window, and French doors. Similar light fixtures are used in the kitchen and dining room. Because the custom cabinets were made of inexpensive wood and then painted, they cost no more than stock stained wood cabinets.

the underside of the sink, covering it completely. Finally, wrap an old piece of carpet around the sides of the disposer housing (back side out), leaving the bottom of the disposer exposed to dissipate heat. Duct tape will hold the carpet in place.

Adding or Replacing a Garbage Disposer

Replacing a garbage disposer is an easy and inexpensive project (not counting the cost of the disposer) that can reduce drain clogging and the noise generated by a worn-out model. Keep in mind, however, that if you are planning to sell your home, purchasing an expensive disposer may not be cost-effective. Most home buyers are more concerned that a disposer exists, not that it has lasting quality and quiet operation.

If you want a disposer that will last, select one with a grinding chamber made of stainless steel. (Most disposers have stainless steel cutting blades but are not all-stainless construction.) Horsepower should be another consideration. The greater the horsepower, the more efficient the disposer. Many disposers are sold without a power cord ("pigtail"). Keep this in mind when you're making price comparisons.

During installation, it is important to knock out the plug at the dishwasher inlet if a dishwasher will be attached. This requirement is true for all disposers. Once you have removed the metal plug, extract it

from the inside of the disposer before running the disposer for the first time.

When installing a new dishwasher or disposer, consider replacing the air gap—the dishwasher air vent device that is usually mounted to one side of the kitchen faucet. The dishwasher drains through the air gap, leaving soap scum and food buildup inside. As a result, old air gaps are usually partially clogged. Because air gaps are inexpensive, it is wise to replace them when you replace the appliance. Air gaps are available in plastic or copper. The latter is more expensive but a far better value.

Adding a Water Purifier

In many areas of the country, a water-purification device is a necessity rather than a luxury. Regardless of the area, however, such a device can make the water safer and more pleasant to drink.

Plumbing-supply stores have a variety of alternatives to under-the-sink and whole-house water purification systems. This do-it-yourself project can be performed for less than one third of the cost of the major water purifiers sold by door-to-door salespeople.

Most small filter systems are used at the cold-water supply only, since hot water is generally used for washing and cooking. Filtering only the cold water is the least expensive option, but filters are available

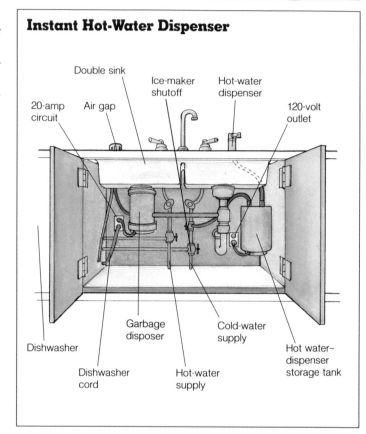

Instant Hot-Water Dispenser

Double sink
Ice-maker shutoff
Hot-water dispenser
20-amp circuit
Air gap
120-volt outlet
Dishwasher
Garbage disposer
Cold-water supply
Hot water–dispenser storage tank
Dishwasher cord
Hot-water supply

that will treat both hot and cold water.

The larger the filter (size is in gallons per minute), the faster the water will flow. A filter that produces a flow of 3½ gallons of water per minute is sufficient for most plumbing fixtures. A smaller and possibly less expensive filter may generate a reduced flow that is annoying to wait for.

Cartridge filters require periodic replacement. Spending 5 to 10 percent more on a unit that has easy-to-replace cartridges can prove to be far more cost-efficient in the long run. Some in-line filters can be a nightmare to replace. To calculate the usable life of the filter, divide the number of gallons used per day into the total number of gallons the filter is rated to clean.

Adding an Instant Hot-Water Dispenser

Tea, instant coffee, instant soup, or any other beverage requiring almost boiling water (180° F) can be as close as the kitchen sink. For a busy family this accessory could prove to be a real time saver.

A hot-water dispenser can be installed into any sink (drilling may be required). Installation is simple: Mount the hot-water tank to the cabinet beneath the sink, connect it to the cold-water supply line, plug it into a 110-volt electrical circuit, and connect it to its own spout mounted alongside the existing kitchen faucet.

New countertops and flooring are medium upgrades with a large impact—on comfort, convenience, and looks. Medium kitchen upgrades cost between $500 and $2,000 and can be completed in two to six days.

Installing Medium-Priced Countertops

Kitchen countertops are commonly constructed from ceramic, marble, or porcelain tile or from plastic laminated onto particleboard or plywood. Countertops can also be made of solid sheeting created from resins (such as Corian®), solid wood (such as maple butcher block), or slab granite or other stone (such as slate). Because a stainless steel work surface is most often used in commercial installations, it will not be discussed in this book.

The two most widely used medium-priced countertop finishes are plastic laminate and ceramic tile. Tile is more resistant to heat, and so it generally lasts longer than laminate. However, tile grout is far more difficult to clean and maintain. Tile is also more expensive to purchase and install.

As is true with all aspects of home improvement, it is wise not to overbuild when it comes to countertops. In a neighborhood where the countertops are predominantly laminate or tile, installing one of the more expensive surface materials, such as Corian® or slab granite, would not be a cost-effective upgrade. However, a small, isolated section of counter or an island cabinet topped with granite or butcher block could lend elegance to a kitchen and would be far more reasonable in cost than a full installation. (See page 53 for expensive countertops.)

Plastic Laminate

Laminate is reasonably resistant to damage, easy to clean and maintain, and relatively inexpensive. Although it can be damaged by hot pots and sharp knives, it is a fine surface for the money.

Many home-improvement centers stock ready-made laminate countertops, and you can save as much as 75 percent of the cost of the overall job by installing the countertop yourself. Usually, ready-made countertops are available in only two or three patterns, and the tops are square-cut on the ends. It takes some skill to make the angle cuts (miters) required to turn corners.

As for custom-cut laminate tops, many small companies specialize in their manufacture, and they will either supply or both supply and install them. When purchasing a custom countertop, it is wise to let the supplier install it, since the price of the counter material is approximately four times the cost of installation, and because the risk of damaging the top during installation is quite high—one slip of a saw could mean damage to the entire top.

The plastic surface of a ready-made top is usually laminated to particleboard, but the most lasting quality is achieved when the plastic is laminated to plywood, since it is more water-resistant than particleboard. The laminate materials themselves also vary in quality. Some laminate has color only on the surface over a black base, whereas solid-color laminate has color that extends all the way through the material, so it isn't as prone to show seams and chips. The selection of solid-color laminates is not as wide as that of surface-color laminates.

Resurfacing a Laminate Countertop With Tile

You can resurface a plastic laminate countertop with tile without removing the countertop. The job is slightly more difficult, but not impossible, if the countertop has rolled edges instead of the square-cut type.

To ensure that the countertop will be waterproof, use epoxy adhesive and epoxy grout. They are more expensive than regular adhesives but are well worth the extra cost.

The tile you select should be made for use on counters. Floor tile is more porous than counter tile and therefore is not as water-resistant; it is also not as resistant to damage by impact as counter tile.

The installation is easy. First, use a saber saw or chisel to cut the connection between the countertop and the back splash. Some damage may occur to adjacent walls and cabinets, so it is wise to plan to retile these areas. Next, use a jigsaw to cut the front edge away from the top. Remove the back splash and front edge, leaving only the horizontal surface. Use a rasp or plane at the front edge to ensure flush alignment with the cabinet below. Next, fill all damaged surfaces in the area to be tiled with a suitable filler. This should include the empty space at the back where the countertop meets the wall.

Getting the sink out of the way is easy. Although you should remove the sink-mount brackets, you need only loosen the plumbing, rather than completely disconnecting it. Use four wood blocks, cut about ⅛ inch thicker than the tile, to hold the sink in place while you install the tile. You can use the same type of bracing to support other built-in appliances, such as a cooktop.

Use a chalk box to mark the tile layout lines. Then spread the adhesive and lay the tile. Do not apply more adhesive than you can cover with tile in a half hour. Also, do not apply the adhesive too thickly, or it won't dry properly. You are using too much adhesive if excess bulges from the joints when you place the tiles. Set the tiles firmly into the adhesive, maintaining an even surface at all times. If a wide joint is desired, use plastic tile spacers to ensure an even installation. Use a straightedge to improve alignment after the tiles are in place.

Ceramic and Porcelain Tile

Both ceramic and porcelain tile are sold in a wide range of colors, sizes, patterns, trim, and surface finishes. Even though some kinds of grout can be a nuisance to maintain, the sleek,

sophisticated look of a properly installed tile countertop provides a high return on investment dollars.

By spending about 20 percent more, you can make inexpensive tile look more appealing by installing it in an interesting way. To achieve the best return on a tile installation, use subtle colors and interesting patterns. You don't have to lay tile in straight horizontal and vertical lines. Installing tile diagonally, staggered in a basket-weave pattern, or in a combination of diagonal and square rows will add value. The use of well-coordinated patterned decorator tiles or a feature strip are other inexpensive additions that can add 30 percent or more to the value of a tile installation.

Porcelain tile lasts longer than ceramic tile because it is far more dense, which makes it more waterproof and resistant to cracking and chipping. Although it is available in a matte finish, porcelain tile is usually known for its super-smooth, extremely high gloss surface. However, it costs 30 to 40 percent more than ceramic tile. Because of cost and lasting quality, porcelain tile is best installed by those planning to stay in their home rather than sell it.

The homeowners kept costs to a minimum in this remodeled kitchen by refacing the original cabinets and using new handles and drawer pulls, removing the old linoleum and sanding and finishing the old fir subfloor, using granite squares rather than slabs on the island countertop and the back splash, and using mixed wood for the wood countertops. New hardware dresses up the original window.

Marble Tile

Countertops made of marble tile are becoming increasingly popular in subdivision as well as custom homes. However, marble is a porous stone that is very easily stained by food and common household chemicals and is nearly impossible to clean. It is wiser to use this luxury material on a bathroom vanity rather than in the kitchen.

Butcher Block

A butcher-block countertop is the most professional cutting and food-preparation surface. However, it should be used sparingly, because wood surfaces require substantial maintenance and discolor easily, and because food is easily trapped in the joints, especially where horizontal surfaces meet vertical ones. An island cabinet countertop, which has no horizontal-to-vertical connection, is an ideal place to use butcher block.

Butcher block is somewhat more expensive than tile and plastic laminate. Maintenance involves sanding every two to three years, combined with regular cleaning and oiling with mineral or vegetable oil.

You can make a butcher-block countertop look far more interesting by using a router to shape the top edge. Avoid a sculptured edge with a pattern, such as an ogee shape (sort of an S), since sanding the top surface might ruin the ogee and require rerouting of the edge.

Adding Major Appliances

Adding or replacing a major appliance is a quick way to modernize a kitchen. Although some replacements might involve a special expense for electrical or gas-line work, today's new appliances are more energy efficient and safer to use than ever before.

The markup on appliances isn't as high as that on light fixtures and furniture. However, purchasing an appliance at a rock-bottom price could prove to be a mistake if the store doesn't have its own delivery, installation, and repair service. In such cases the store usually advises the customer to bring the item back for a replacement or to contact the manufacturer for a warranty repair. In either case, extra costs are involved.

The least expensive appliance replacement is one that fits exactly into the space in the existing cabinets. Modifying a cabinet can sometimes cost more than twice as much as the appliance itself, as can modifying the electrical or gas service.

All appliances have installation instructions and specification sheets. It is wise to review these documents carefully before making a purchase.

Many types of appliances are available with key locks that can prevent use by small children. In addition, electrical cooktops are available that generate heat only when special cookware is placed on the surface.

Converting to a Gas Range or Gas Cooktop

Gas appliances provide instant heat, and modern ones are more energy efficient and burn cleaner than outdated ones. However, converting from an electric cooktop or range to a gas one can be expensive even if the new appliance will fit perfectly into the old space.

Range Venting Options

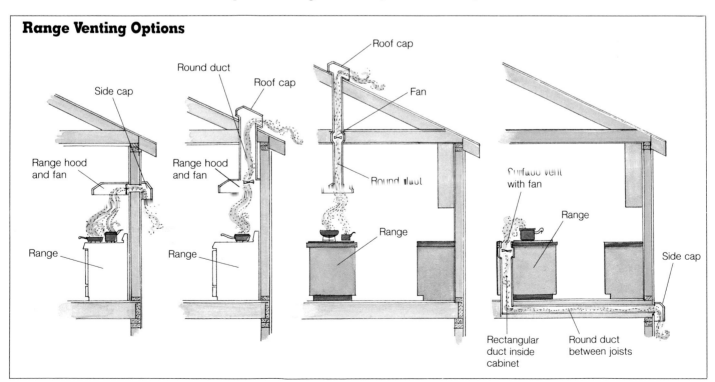

Side cap

Range hood and fan

Range

Round duct

Roof cap

Range hood and fan

Range

Roof cap

Fan

Round duct

Range

Surface vent with fan

Range

Side cap

Rectangular duct inside cabinet

Round duct between joists

Three important costs to consider are that of extending the gas line, upgrading the exhaust hood, and providing 110-volt power. (Modern gas ranges use a small amount of electricity for panel lights and automatic ignition and shutdown systems.)

Gas appliances are rated by volume of gas, expressed in British thermal units (BTUs). When a house is first built, gas lines are sized according to the number of BTUs each appliance will use. Although the main gas line from the street may be sufficient to supply fuel to more appliances, the feeder pipes that travel to the individual appliances may not be large enough to supply gas to a second appliance.

Tapping into a gas line that isn't large enough to fuel both the existing appliance and a new one could mean flame-out and a possible fire or explosion. (In many older appliances, gas will continue to flow when the flame has been extinguished.) Most licensed plumbing contractors are capable of properly sizing a gas line. Do-it-yourselfers who are not familiar with gas lines should hire a professional for this portion of the project.

Gas ranges generate more exhaust than electrical appliances do. In addition to the steam produced from the food being cooked, the flame also generates unwanted and potentially dangerous fumes. For this reason the Uniform Building Code requires that range hoods for gas appliances exhaust more cubic feet of air per minute (cfm) than those for the same size electrical cooking appliances. With gas appliances it is not wise to use recirculating range hoods, because they filter the gases but do not exhaust them to the outside.

Caution: Newly installed gas lines should be pressure-tested for leaks. Using soapy water at each joint as the only test is not an acceptable method. To test the line properly, cap the pipe at the appliance location, install a pressure test gauge at the point where the new pipe will be connected to the existing pipe, and then fill the new pipe with compressed air. If the pressurized pipe leaks, a drop in pressure will show on the gauge. Then, use soapy water to find the leaks. Once these are corrected, retest the line. Finally, after connecting the appliance and the new pipe, use soapy water again to test for leaks. If new gas valves will be used in the configuration, they should be connected during the pressure test. (Even new gas valves frequently leak.)

Installing Floor Coverings

Properly preparing an old floor for a new covering is an important factor in achieving the most cost-effective result, regardless of the type of replacement covering.

Covering old kitchen flooring with another layer is not recommended; the most important reason being the possibility of not discovering hidden water damage to the subfloor. There are only a few instances in the life of a home when the subfloor can be inspected, and there isn't a more cost-effective time than during replacement of the floor covering.

The only case in which glued-on finish flooring is attached directly to a structural floor is when the floor is made of concrete. On wood floors, the new finish flooring is glued to an intermediate layer of plywood or particleboard, called underlayment. First, staple the underlayment to the wood subfloor. Then putty the joints and staple holes with a smoothing compound. Finally, glue the flooring to the underlayment. You can then remove the flooring later by prying up the underlayment without damaging the subfloor, which is expensive to replace.

Always replace the underlayment when installing vinyl floors, whether tile or sheet; adding a half-inch layer of vinyl and underlayment over an existing layer will thicken the flooring layer and can cause problems later if you need to remove a built-in appliance. Omitting the underlayment can cause another complication: When a new layer of vinyl is installed over an existing layer without underlayment, the surface texture of the old flooring can transfer through to the new layer, in many cases distorting the new surface in less than a month. If the old floor is perfectly smooth, no texture will pass through to a new layer. But if the old floor is not securely attached to its substrate, the new floor will also be loose, no matter how well it is glued to the old layer.

When reflooring, first remove all appliances, the existing floor covering, and the underlayment. Check for damage to the subfloor, make all necessary repairs, and then install the new underlayment and floor covering. Replacing the flooring from the underlayment up (excluding repairs due to water damage) will cost an extra 15 to 20 percent, but your peace of mind and the finished appearance will make the additional cost worthwhile.

Ceramic Tile

Covering a wood subfloor with tile is not a simple task, but it can greatly improve the value of a home. With tile, the most cost-effective installation is the one that will last the longest. Improperly installed tile will not last.

Laying tile on a concrete floor that's in good condition poses no special problems, but houses with wood subfloors are another story. Wood floors flex and ceramic tile is brittle, so you must stiffen the wood floor before applying the tile to keep the tile from cracking. The strengthening process should be performed from above and below the floor. Below the floor, add additional supports to completely eliminate movement of the floor frame. This is hard work, and it is expensive.

Once you have braced the horizontal floor-framing members, you must then prevent the subfloor from flexing. You

Installing Floor Tile

Cutting Tiles

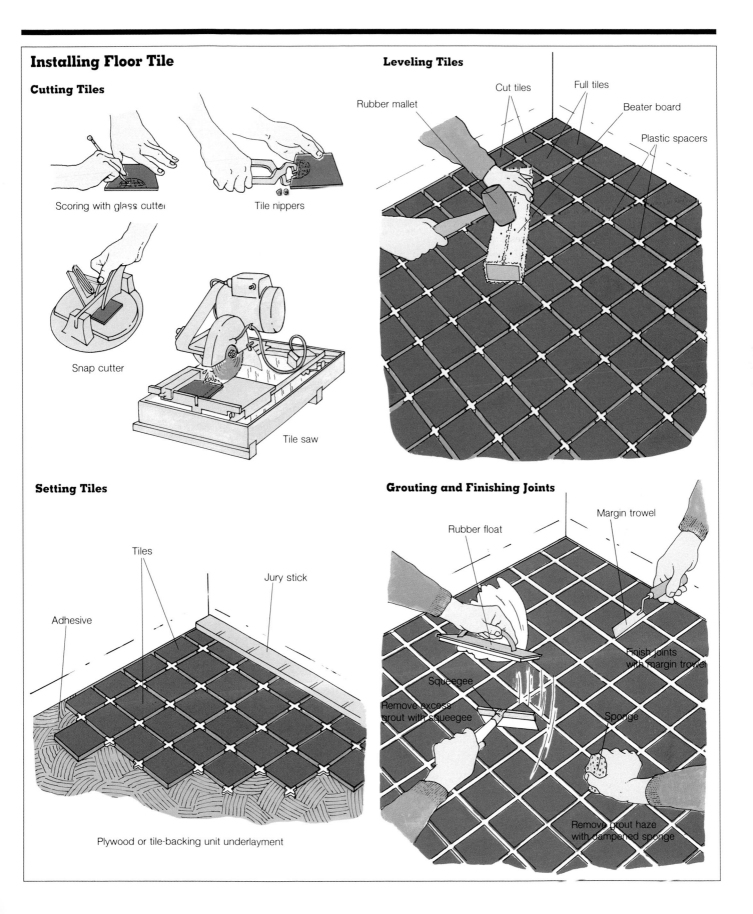

Scoring with glass cutter

Tile nippers

Snap cutter

Tile saw

Leveling Tiles

Rubber mallet

Cut tiles

Full tiles

Beater board

Plastic spacers

Setting Tiles

Tiles

Jury stick

Adhesive

Plywood or tile-backing unit underlayment

Grouting and Finishing Joints

Rubber float

Margin trowel

Finish joints with margin trowel

Squeegee

Remove excess grout with squeegee

Sponge

Remove grout haze with dampened sponge

can accomplish this by applying a ¾-inch-thick to 1-inch-thick layer of mortar onto the surface of the subfloor. The mortar adds the strength required to keep the subfloor from flexing and at the same time smooths irregularities common in wood subfloors. It is very important to install tile over a smooth substrate. It is also important to make sure that the finished thickness of the new floor—mortar and tile combined—is as close as possible in height to any adjacent floor coverings.

Vinyl Tile

One-foot-square vinyl tile is the floor covering of choice for most do-it-yourselfers. There are two basic types of vinyl tile—glue-on and self-sticking. The self-sticking type is easier to install but doesn't last as long as tile installed with a proper adhesive. Part of good adhesion is derived from moist glue penetrating the surface of the substrate. This process cannot occur properly with self-sticking products. In addition, there is no adhesive below the joints of self-sticking tiles, making the substrate more susceptible to water damage.

Using too much glue when installing glue-on vinyl tiles can be as unsightly as not using enough. Excessive amounts of glue can take months to dry and will cause the tiles to bulge and buckle; the excess glue will ooze out through the joints for months after the floor is completed.

The trick to a good installation is a thin layer of adhesive. Allow it to cure for about 30 minutes before applying the tiles. Completing small areas at a time will make the job easier to manage.

Sheet Vinyl

The most popular vinyl surface is sheet vinyl, or linoleum. It has fewer seams than individual tile installations, it is more resistant to water damage, and it can be coved up the wall for greater protection against water damage. In addition, the almost jointless installation is easier to clean and maintain. The one drawback is that a proper installation requires specialized talent.

When replacing a floor with sheet vinyl, it is important to consider how many seams will be required and where the seams will be located. Regardless of the number of seams, they should be as far away from heavily trafficked areas as possible. If you select a 6-foot-wide material to cover a floor that is 9 feet wide, expect to have a seam. Although 12-foot-wide material can be a solution to the problem, it may not be available in the desired pattern.

In many instances good planning can reduce the number of seams required without increasing cost, but in most cases fewer seams mean higher cost. However, the floor will last longer, which makes it the most cost-effective installation in the long run.

Caution: Inexpensive cushioned-back vinyls are best used in bathrooms, laundry rooms, and closets. Since they are highly susceptible to damage, they are not recommended for use in kitchens or other heavily trafficked areas.

Adding a Garden Window

You can enhance and brighten your kitchen by replacing a standard window with a specialty unit, such as a garden window. At the same time, you can improve energy efficiency by using double- or triple-pane glass. Multiple layers of glass filled with argon gas are even more efficient. In a high-glare situation, reflective glass can be useful.

More light enters a room through a garden window than a standard window of the same size because the side and top panes of a garden window protrude beyond the exterior wall of the home, allowing light to enter the room from more than one direction.

A garden window is especially cost-efficient to install if an available stock size fits into the existing opening, so that no special wall reconstruction is required. Many stock sizes are available. In this situation, installing a garden window, especially a small one, may qualify as a small upgrade. When an existing opening is nonstandard and a custom size must be ordered, or when you need a large standard-sized window,

this project is a medium upgrade. Many manufacturers will make custom sizes for about 15 percent more than the cost of similar stock sizes.

It is important to retrofit a window properly; the manufacturer's installation guide provides a number of good tips. Proper flashing and caulking are imperative, since leaks are a common problem with incorrect installations.

The following are a few important considerations for deciding which brand of window to purchase. First, for maximum cost efficiency, it is important to ensure that the window fits exactly into the existing opening. Next, consider how the window opens. Some have operable sections on the sides, and others open on the top. In either case, ease of operation should be the major concern.

Although one or two brands have aluminum bottom panels, the bottom panel of most garden windows is made from some type of wood (regular plywood, particleboard, or marine plywood). If you will be placing houseplants in the window, a bottom panel constructed from marine plywood will best withstand water damage.

If a brand has all the features you desire, but the bottom panel is not waterproof, you can paint the wood with a coat of fiberglass resin. Although it will add slightly to the initial cost, the resin will reduce the possibility of moisture deterioration, and the window will last much longer.

Properly planned and completed in stages, even a major renovation can be minimally disruptive, so that you will still have a place to store dishes, to cook, and to serve meals. Large upgrades cost more than $2,000, although some can be completed in a day or two.

Installing Hardwood Flooring

The first question a prospective buyer asks about a hardwood floor is, "Is it hard to clean?"

Bumpy, grooved, plugged, and notched hardwood flooring is not practical for the kitchen. Although it may look good in the showroom, it doesn't hold up well to moisture and food spills. Use a square-edged, flush-jointed style in the kitchen, and take special care to ensure tight joints between planks on all four sides.

There are two types of prefinished hardwood flooring—solid planks and veneered plywood planks. The latter are highly susceptible to damage from falling objects and once damaged are nearly impossible to repair. Solid planks resist most kinds of abuse and can be refinished again and again. Solid-plank hardwood costs 30 to 50 percent more than veneered plywood planks but will last 10 times longer.

For lasting quality, take two precautions when installing hardwood. First, always use a vapor barrier between the subfloor and the hardwood flooring boards. Second, never glue the hardwood directly to the subfloor. The correct way to attach prefinished hardwood floors is to nail a layer of underlayment to the subfloor and then glue the hardwood to the underlayment.

The finest hardwood floor is the custom floor. It is nailed directly to the subfloor over a moisture barrier, then it is puttied, sanded, stained, and varnished in place. This type of hardwood floor is the most water-resistant and easiest to clean. Even though it is the most expensive, it is also the longest lasting, which makes it the most cost-effective type of flooring.

Installing Expensive Countertops

Expensive countertop materials, such as Corian® and slab marble and granite, can be stunning additions to a kitchen. Their durability and ease of maintenance complement their exceptional beauty.

Corian® is a popular synthetic countertop material that is durable and stain resistant; in addition, accidental cuts can be repaired by sanding. Corian® and similar synthetic products are popular in finer homes; they cost approximately 35 percent more than ceramic tile and about five times as much as plastic laminate. For an interesting look, trim synthetic countertops with a ceramic tile back splash, and use wood or metal trim for an unusual edge detail.

Synthetic slab countertops made of cultured marble, cultured onyx, and cultured granite are better used in bathrooms than in the kitchen, since they are easily stained by food and beverages and are less durable than Corian® and similar synthetics.

Natural slab granite is durable, beautiful, unique, and expensive. A granite countertop will not provide much of a return in a first-time-buyer's neighborhood, but it can be considered a sensible investment in move-up homes.

Granite is available in a wide range of prices, depending upon the type used and how it will be edged. Some types are more widely available than others, making them less expensive. The slabs are usually ¾ inch thick but are made to look thicker by having a second piece glued onto the underside of the front edge. Polishing can make the seam almost invisible to the naked eye.

Installing a Bow Window

Adding a bow window at the kitchen sink can turn a small, plain kitchen into a light, airy, spacious-looking one. The project is relatively expensive, but if a room addition is out of the question and the kitchen is cramped, a bow window could be the most cost-effective alternative.

Bow windows differ from bay windows in that they have four or more panels. Bay

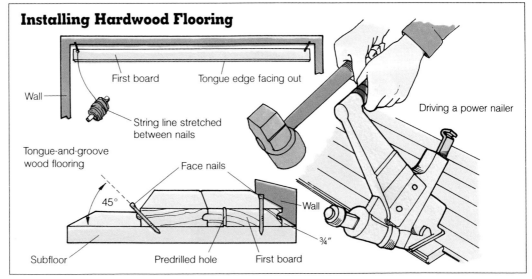

Installing Hardwood Flooring

First board
Tongue edge facing out
Wall
String line stretched between nails
Tongue-and-groove wood flooring
Driving a power nailer
45°
Face nails
Wall
Subfloor
Predrilled hole
First board
¾"

windows have three (see pages 84 and 93). Bow windows are available in aluminum, vinyl, wood, and clad wood frames. Cladding is available in aluminum or vinyl. It is important to use a frame material that matches that of the rest of the windows in the house. A wood-framed window installed in a house with aluminum frames might look out of place and could actually diminish the value of the home.

Installation cost is the main reason that a bow window is more expensive than other types of specialty windows. Structural alterations are usually necessary. This project should

be planned with the help of an architect or a designer and a contractor or an engineer.

Loss of usable wall space is a drawback to a bow window. If the bow window is wider than the window being replaced, the opening in the wall will have to be enlarged. Reduced wall space also might result in the loss of wall cabinets. Consider these trade-offs carefully. You might decide to install a skylight instead.

Installing a Skylight

A skylight can add natural light and, with some models, ventilation to an otherwise dark and

Skylights and casement windows brighten this remodeled eat-in kitchen. Other new touches include recessed lights in the eating area, hardwood floors, and an appliance garage.

dreary work place without diminishing wall space.

A skylight itself is relatively inexpensive, but installation can involve costly structural alterations. Plan the installation with the assistance of a professional. This is important because proper installation is necessary to reduce the chance of leaks. Skylights themselves don't usually leak. Most often, leaks occur at a faulty joint between the skylight and the roof.

The installer should use connection details provided by the National Roofing Contractors Association in its *Roofing & Waterproofing Manual* (see page 108). The installation information provided with the skylight may not be sufficient to ensure a watertight configuration with every type of roofing material.

Metal flashings are usually required for the installation. Some skylight companies offer the flashing at extra charge; if they don't, a heating and sheet-metal contractor can make them. Some tile roofs require lead flashing for a proper seal, which can be expensive. Roofing contractors are expert in this area.

Do not use canned roof patching compound (a cold patch) to install a skylight in a hot-asphalt type of roof. The connection will not last and eventually a leak will occur. Use hot asphalt for a more permanent seal, even though it is more expensive initially.

Installing a skylight in the kitchen is somewhat different from installing one in most other rooms, mainly because the kitchen requires more artificial lighting in the ceiling, which

leaves less space available for a skylight. During the planning phase it is important to consider rearranging rather than eliminating any artifical lighting.

There are two basic types of skylights—fixed and operable. A fixed skylight (one that doesn't open) is the least expensive of the two. It is available with either a domed plastic lens or a flat glass lens. Of these two, the domed plastic lens is the least expensive and most commonly used.

Operable skylights, sometimes called skywindows, can be opened and come in a wide variety of styles. Some open only on the side to improve ventilation; others lift open. Some can be opened and closed manually; others have electrical controls. Some electrically operated models have moisture sensors that will close the skylight automatically in the event of wet weather. Louvered blinds to reduce heat and light on hot days are another option; the blinds in some models open and close electrically.

Refacing Cabinets

Advertisements claim that cabinet refacing can be done for 50 percent of the cost of replacement, and it's true. It's also true that a refaced surface, done properly, will last a long time and be worth the price. However, replacement, not refacing, is best if you are planning to remodel your kitchen completely and if the existing cabinet space is arranged inefficiently.

All appliances must be removed before refacing can

begin. Then remove moldings, drawers, blank drawer fronts, and doors and hinges. Rough the remaining surfaces with sandpaper (50 to 80 grit), and apply a layer of contact cement. Also coat the back of the veneer to be used for refacing with contact cement. Allow the cement to dry, and then press the veneer onto the cabinet surfaces and trim the edges with a router, razor knife, file, and sandpaper. If plastic laminate is the veneer of choice, paint the cabinet interiors before beginning the refacing process. Next, install new moldings, doors, and drawer fronts. Finally, if the veneer is wood, you can either apply stain and varnish, or paint.

A good refacing job requires lump-free adhesive application and careful trimming of the newly applied veneer. Grained veneers should be applied so that the grain runs in the same direction, usually vertically, except on horizontal rails.

Replacing Cabinets

Cabinet replacement is most cost-effective when you are completely remodeling the kitchen. Damage to cabinets and countertops is most likely during the removal required for most major kitchen remodeling.

As has been noted previously, the markup on prefabricated (modular) cabinets is high, so when shopping for modular units, expect 50 to 70 percent discounts. This is not true for custom cabinets, although prices will vary greatly from cabinetmaker to cabinetmaker, depending on quality of construction, accessories, door style, and finish. Not every cabinetmaker is a good designer. Professional design assistance is most important to achieve a high-quality finished product.

Dovetailed drawer construction is the finest, but its

The delicate floral trim in this kitchen is repeated in the wallcovering and matching fabric, the tile back splash, and the island countertop trim. Note the electric power strip on the island and the refrigerator faced to match the cabinetry.

Kitchen Cabinet Layout

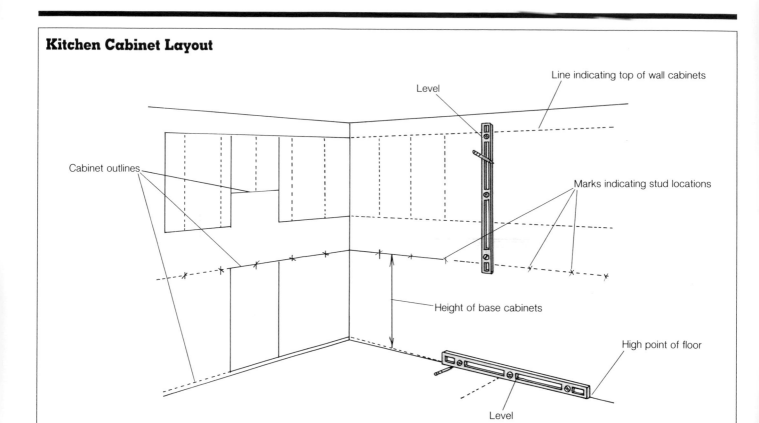

Level

Line indicating top of wall cabinets

Cabinet outlines

Marks indicating stud locations

Height of base cabinets

High point of floor

Level

Wall Cabinet Installation

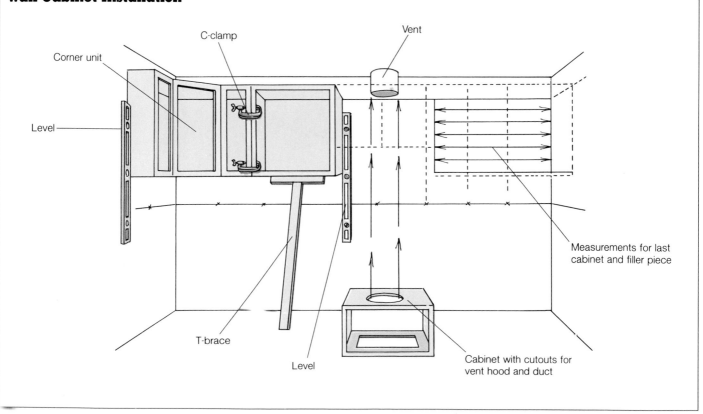

C-clamp

Vent

Corner unit

Level

Measurements for last cabinet and filler piece

T-brace

Level

Cabinet with cutouts for vent hood and duct

Base Cabinet Installation

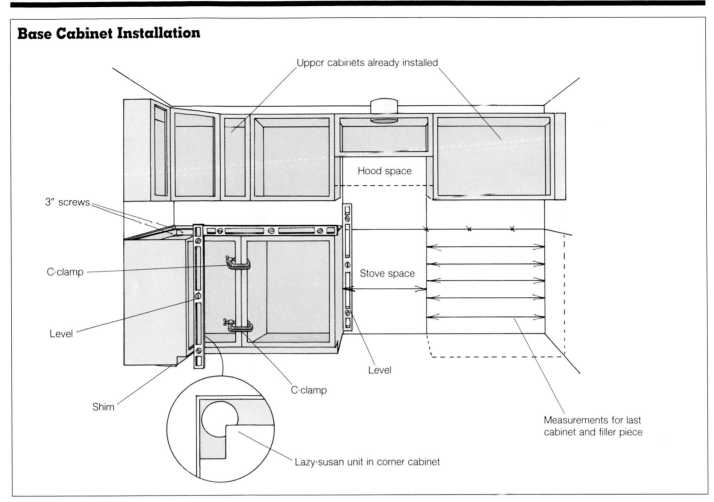

Upper cabinets already installed

Hood space

3" screws

C-clamp

Level

Shim

Stove space

Level

C-clamp

Lazy-susan unit in corner cabinet

Measurements for last cabinet and filler piece

absence should not preclude the importance of strong hardware (drawer glides and hinges), thick cabinet walls, finished interiors, good-quality wood products and accessories, and a fine finish.

Factory-applied varnishes are usually superior to those on locally made cabinets. However cabinets with photo-finished" surfaces, such as contact paper, are not a good investment.

Adding Island Cabinets

Island cabinets can make a kitchen more versatile and interesting. It is important when installing them to avoid creating tight passageways. To find out how well an island cabinet would work in an existing kitchen, try the following. Measure a point 3 feet in front of the dishwasher and place a kitchen chair on the mark. Open the dishwasher, bend over, and pull out the bottom tray. If your body doesn't bump the chair, you have enough space to install an island. Perform this experiment with any appliances that will open into a walkway created by the installation of an island cabinet.

Remodeling or Expanding a Kitchen

Statistics show that you can expect a 75 to 110 percent return on your investment from a kitchen remodeling project, with expansions returning slightly less. This excellent return compounds the pleasure of having a safe, luxurious, modern work center.

No home improvement is more satisfying than a complete renovation. But the process can be stressful. You can minimize the stress by making as many decisions as possible before the project begins, preparing a separate cooking and

sink area to be used during construction, and accepting that your life will be in disarray for many weeks.

The success of a kitchen remodeling project or expansion depends on planning. Every detail must be thoroughly studied. Making a wants and needs checklist of every feature in the new kitchen can make planning easier. Architects, designers, and contractors can get a better idea about your dream kitchen by knowing your preferences.

THE BATHROOM

No other room in the house is subject to more use by everyone in the family than the bathroom. Whereas most other rooms are improved for comfort and convenience, many bathroom improvements have become necessities due to changes in life-style. One bathroom is rarely sufficient for an entire family, especially when it must accommodate two income earners in the morning, not to mention children getting ready for school.

The addition of a second bathroom to a one-bath home is the most cost-effective bathroom upgrade. Yet it may not be affordable or high enough on the list of priorities to justify doing at first. In that case, the second most cost-effective improvement is remodeling a bathroom to make it more convenient for two people to use at one time. Remodeling can mean anything from installing a new light fixture to replacing a toilet to adding a second sink. The latter can greatly alleviate the rush to get ready for work in the morning.

A rimless shower door, louvered shutters, brass and ceramic fixtures, and skylights with sensors that close automatically in the rain add distinction, function, and style to this remodeled bathroom.

For a homeowner who is handy, the cost of some small bathroom upgrades can be less than a night out at the movies for the family. Like all the small upgrades in this book, small bathroom projects cost up to $500 and can be completed in a day or two.

Installing a Mirror

A mirror can create the illusion of space in a small bathroom. Large mirrors enhance the light in the room and reflect its various finishes, creating beauty and interest. Polished or beveled edges, etched borders, curves, and layered glass make mirrors a dramatic and elegant accessory.

A mirror need not be limited to the space over the sink or vanity. It can wrap a vanity on all sides. It can run from the top of the counter or counter back splash to the ceiling. It can be framed in decorative metal trim to match other finishes in the bathroom.

Caution: Avoid installing a mirror directly on a surface where there may be standing water. The silver coating on the back of the mirror will be damaged by continued contact with dampness or moisture. This is especially true when decorative J-molding is used at the bottom of the mirror to hold it in place. Water can become trapped in this channel, permanently damaging the mirror. Instead, install the mirror in a bed of panel adhesive or with conventional mirror clips.

You can purchase precut mirrors at most hardware stores and home-improvement centers. If the design you desire varies from the norm even a bit, however, a custom mirror will be required. Custom mirrors are available from companies specializing in mirror fabrication or glass replacement. Rounded edges, bevels, and other special cuts will add significantly to the purchase price.

Installing a Medicine Cabinet

Medicine cabinets are as attractive as they are useful and are sold in an almost limitless number of shapes and sizes. Many are much larger than old-fashioned cabinets, and some of the more expensive models have interiors as fancy as their exteriors. Options include mirrors inside and out, integral lighting and electrical outlets, swing-out magnifying mirrors, and even a mirror defogger. You can choose swinging or sliding doors, recessed or surface-mounted models, and interchangeable configurations.

If you choose a recessed model that is larger than your current medicine cabinet, you can alter the existing opening,

Bathroom Upgrades

For an overview of the bathroom, before and after remodeling, see pages 6 and 7.

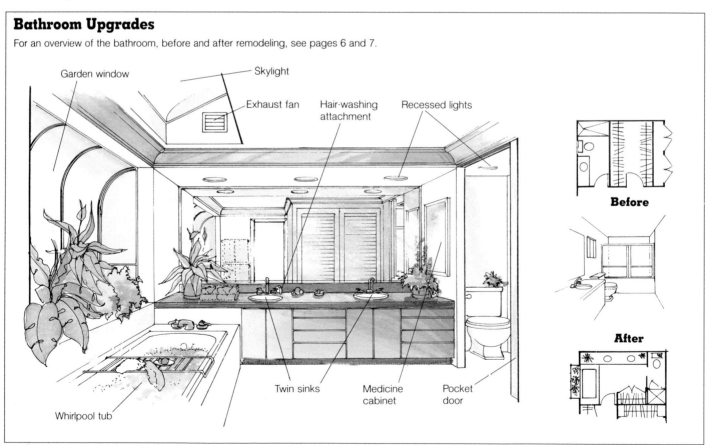

Garden window

Skylight

Exhaust fan

Hair-washing attachment

Recessed lights

Whirlpool tub

Twin sinks

Medicine cabinet

Pocket door

Before

After

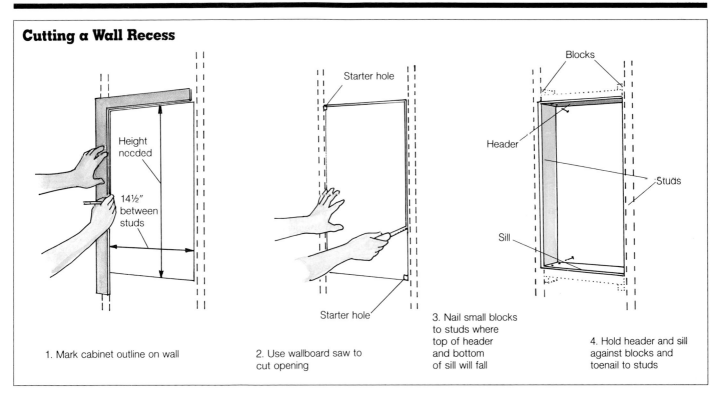

Cutting a Wall Recess

1. Mark cabinet outline on wall

Height needed

14½" between studs

2. Use wallboard saw to cut opening

Starter hole

Starter hole

3. Nail small blocks to studs where top of header and bottom of sill will fall

Blocks

Header

Studs

Sill

4. Hold header and sill against blocks and toenail to studs

provided that there is no plumbing, electrical, or mechanical equipment inside the wall. If there is, it may be preferable both in terms of cost and disruption to install a surface-mounted cabinet.

Medicine cabinets range widely in price, depending upon the size and the number of features. Elaborate models fall outside the range of a small upgrade, but even the most difficult configurations can usually be installed in less than a day.

Replacing a Toilet or Seat

Apart from aesthetic considerations, one of the primary reasons for replacing a toilet is to save water. Replacing a toilet is a lot like trading in a car for a new one. The old car may run satisfactorily, but a new model is certainly more stylish and generally more efficient.

Toilets are sold in an enormous number of brands, styles, and colors. The least costly and most common are two-piece, or close-coupled, toilets. The most stylish and most expensive are one-piece, or low-profile, toilets, some of which may be beyond the range of a small upgrade. Two-piece toilets depend a great deal on gravity; one-piece models contain sophisticated entrails that facilitate a full yet quiet flush with a minimal amount of water.

Water conservation is an excellent reason to replace an old toilet with a modern, more efficient model. Many older toilets use between 5 and 7 gallons of water per flush; modern, water-saving models use about 3.5 gallons per flush. New legislation in many states requires the manufacture and installation of ultra-low-flow (ULF) toilets that use 1.5 gallons per flush. Many ULF toilets contain devices that assist the flush with air.

Replacing an old, worn toilet seat will improve the appearance of any bathroom. A screwdriver, a pair of pliers, and about 20 minutes are all that you need to perform this task.

Most toilet seats are manufactured from wood, wood by-products, or plastics. Those made from plastic are more expensive, offer excellent lasting quality, and come in a wide range of colors and styles. Those made from wood, such as natural oak, are most appropriate with traditional or colonial decor.

Replacing a Tub Enclosure

A tub enclosure that is leaking and does not contain safety glass is a candidate for replacement. One major reason that many people do not have a tub enclosure is their fear of being

severely cut in a fall. This is no longer a problem with modern tub enclosures, which are constructed with safety glass—essentially the same type of glass used in automobiles. It is designed to fracture into small, nonjagged pieces that will remain connected and not cause injury.

Many frame styles and finishes are available for tub enclosures. Frameless tub enclosures with clear glass are especially effective if the goal is to minimize visual distractions or to make a smaller bathroom seem bigger. If privacy is a concern, many opaque or translucent glass patterns are available, or you may choose to have custom etched glass panels fabricated.

Replacing a Faucet

Now more then ever, a bathroom faucet must not only be functional but must look good

Replacing a Faucet

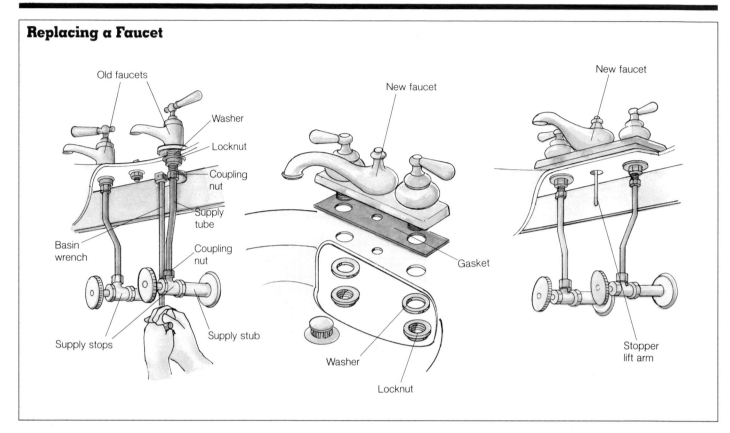

Old faucets
Washer
Locknut
Coupling nut
Supply tube
Basin wrench
Coupling nut
Supply stops
Supply stub
New faucet
Gasket
Washer
Locknut
New faucet
Stopper lift arm

too. There is an enormous variety of faucet styles and finishes, ranging widely in quality and price. Replacing a faucet is a medium upgrade that should take a couple of hours.

Look for a faucet whose body and working parts are constructed of solid brass. Although you will find many inexpensive faucets constructed of plastic or other synthetic materials, the finish will last significantly longer on more expensive brass faucets. All of the major American plumbing companies offer a wide selection of superior faucets and **valves** that not only provide longevity, but will maintain their attractive appearance for years.

When replacing a faucet, you may want to consider installing a hair-washing sprayer. This device is available as an optional accessory with many

of the leading lavatory faucets and can be a real bonus. Hair-washing sprayers come with installation accessories and can be installed in about an hour.

Replacing a Sink

If the new faucet you just bought makes your old sink look even worse, you might want to replace the sink. Among the other reasons you might find for justifying this upgrade is that after countless hours of searching for just the right faucet, it's fairly common to find that the one selected has an 8-inch centerset (the distance from the center of the hot-water faucet to the center of the cold-water faucet), and the existing sink will accept only a 4-inch centerset. Also, a hair-washing attachment needs an additional hole drilled, and

a bigger sink makes hair washing easier.

Material and style are two considerations when shopping for a new sink. The options for the material include enameled steel, enameled cast iron, vitreous china, acrylic, teak, pottery, and even hammered brass. The style options include round, oval, square, hexagonal, shell shaped, and even a specially designed hair-washing sink.

Enameled cast iron or vitreous china are probably the most cost-effective options. They are not the most competitively priced but will wear significantly better than any of the other choices.

Since finding a replacement sink to match a countertop exactly is difficult (almost impossible if the sink or countertop is more than 10 years old), consider using a complementary color. If you have selected a

self-rimming sink, see page 36 for a few tips on installing it.

Refinishing Fixtures

One cost-effective way to give a bathroom a fresh, new look is to refinish the bathtub, sink, and toilet. It's a simple process: The fixture is chemically cleaned and etched, and then a porcelainlike finish is applied. The new finish is cured with heat or chemicals and then thoroughly polished.

The finish is either a polyurethane enamel or an epoxy; the former lasts about five years, the latter can discolor in about six months, so be sure to ask about a warranty. Also, do not consider refinishing if the structure surrounding the fixture is damaged. In such cases, it is necessary to remove the fixture to make a more complete investigation of what exists and what proper repairs should be made.

Refinishing is a smart alternative to replacement if the fixture enamel or fiberglass is worn off, stained, or moderately chipped. Refinishing does not require the removal of the surrounding wallcoverings, such as tile and wallpaper, whereas fixture replacement does. For example, refinishing an existing tub would cost about one tenth of the price of replacing a tub that is surrounded by ceramic tile, including the tile work, plumbing labor, and the cost of the new tub itself.

Another advantage of refinishing is the minimal level of disruption. Refinishing usually takes only a day or two, whereas replacement, including plumbing, wallboard, tile, and so forth, could easily take a couple of weeks.

Refinishing is not limited to fixtures. Many firms will apply the same finish to ceramic tile. However, refinishing damaged tile can mask other more serious problems in the substrate, which could result in heftier costs down the road. If the color of the tile is the problem, you will be dollars ahead by simply removing it and replacing it with something new, since unlike fixture refinishing, tile refinishing tends to diminish the cosmetic value of the tile.

If you do decide to refinish the tile, clean it meticulously with a bathtub cleaning product and a dish-scrubbing pad. You may even find it necessary to regrout the tile, which in itself will greatly enhance both its appearance and integrity.

Installing a Washbasin

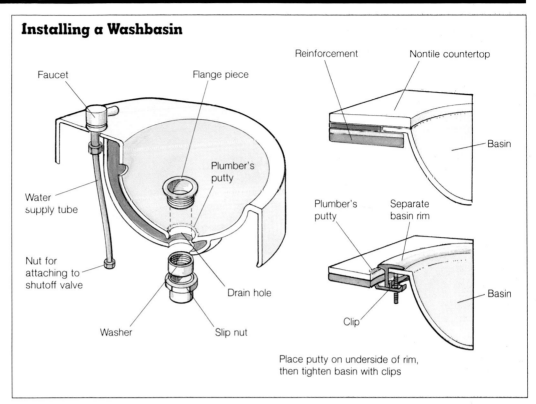

Faucet

Flange piece

Reinforcement

Nontile countertop

Water supply tube

Plumber's putty

Basin

Nut for attaching to shutoff valve

Plumber's putty

Separate basin rim

Washer

Drain hole

Slip nut

Clip

Basin

Place putty on underside of rim, then tighten basin with clips

Applying Wallcoverings

Few projects offer more return on an investment than new wallcoverings or a fresh coat of paint. By the same token, if not done properly, there are few things that can do more to spoil the look of the space. Both of these projects can be done without the help of a professional. Plan on spending a weekend's worth of your time, most of which will involve wall preparation.

The wallcovering you select for a bathroom should withstand considerable moisture. Although you can use foil and plain-paper wallcoverings, the best bet for long-term adhesion and easy cleanup is a vinyl wallcovering.

Before installing the wallcovering, make sure that the walls are smooth and free of imperfections, since these blemishes will be more apparent after the wallpaper is hung. Smooth walls that are textured with 80-grit sandpaper and a sanding block. Fill low spots with joint compound or vinyl patching compound. For a smoother finish, coat the entire wall from floor to ceiling with joint compound applied with an 8- to 12-inch putty knife. Once dry, sand the compound to ensure a uniform finish.

Seal the walls designated for covering with at least one coat of an oil-based primer. This will minimize the amount of moisture that the wallboard absorbs, making the wallcovering easier to manage during installation and significantly easier to remove in the future.

Because of the amount of heat and moisture generated in a bathroom, it is especially important to ensure adequate adhesion by applying paste to the wallcovering, even if it is prepasted. To protect against the growth of mildew and other fungi, use a mildew-resistant paste.

Adding a Light Fixture

Lighting contributes to both the comfort and safety of a bathroom. It is designed to emphasize the myriad colors and textures in a modern bathroom.

Start this improvement by assessing where additional lighting may be needed: over a tub or shower, over a vanity or dressing table, or just to enhance the space as a whole. Call an electrician if you are not handy or you don't feel confident enough about this project.

Recessed lights offer a clean, unobtrusive look that will highlight a specific area, adding interest and excellent illumination. Those used in certain parts of the bathroom must be approved for use around dampness and moisture and are fitted with a special waterproof trim for added protection. Most manufacturers of recessed lights offer a retrofit model, which can be installed in an existing ceiling if there is attic space above to allow for the installation of wires running from the new light location to a switch in the wall. If the room is located between floors, you will need to remove at least part of the ceiling to install the wires. In this case, retrofit housings will not be required.

Surface-mounted ceiling lighting is not as popular as it once was, but it is still an alternative. Here, the simpler the style the better. Surface-mounted ceiling lighting offers good general lighting but is not as effective as recessed lights for specific tasks, such as bathing, shaving, or applying cosmetics.

The basic wiring for surface-mounted ceiling lighting is the same as that for recessed lighting except that you will need to install a light rough-in box instead of the recessed light housing. Some additional blocking between the joists may also be required to support the fixture adequately.

One way to improve the general lighting in the bathroom is with a combination exhaust fan and light. These are generally more expensive to install than a plain light fixture because, in addition to the added electrical work, the fan housing must be vented to the exterior. These units also frequently require more than one switch, which also adds to the cost.

The cost of an above-average exhaust fan and light combination depends on the amount of air it will move and the level of noise it emits. The larger, quieter units are the most expensive but are well worth the added cost in comfort and convenience. With professional installation, this project could qualify as a medium upgrade.

Replacing a Light Fixture

Many bathrooms have a small light fixture mounted on the wall directly above the mirrored medicine cabinet. The light casts shadows on the face, which makes it difficult to shave or apply makeup. A better solution is lights mounted on either side of the mirror.

Although replacing a light fixture doesn't require the skills of a licensed electrician, you should use extreme caution when performing this task. The best place to begin this project is at a hardware store, home-improvement center, or lighting specialty store. Do this before removing the existing fixture. Most of these stores have qualified lighting consultants on their staff. It is helpful to supply them with a photograph or simple sketch of your bathroom that clearly reflects what exists. This will enable the consultant to make specific suggestions regarding the size, style, and finish of the replacement fixture.

Maintaining an Exhaust Fan

Many people who already have an exhaust fan don't use it because it either is too noisy or isn't in good working order. The former is usually a result of the latter.

The first step in fan maintenance is to turn off the circuit breaker that supplies power to the fan. Then, and only then, remove the protective grille that conceals the fan and housing. Thoroughly vacuum all the parts to remove any dust, dirt, and dead insects. These not only make the fan less efficient, they contribute to its early demise. Apply a couple of drops of fine machine oil to the shaft to ensure that it will operate smoothly. Then clean the grille with a solution of ammonia and warm water. Replace the grille before turning the circuit breaker back on.

A polyurethane enamel refinishing adds at least five years of life to this bathtub.

Installing Safety Devices

A ground fault circuit interrupter (GFCI) will prevent serious shock. This is especially important in the bathroom, where electrical appliances are used in close proximity to water. See page 40 for more information on this safety upgrade.

One of the most dangerous places in the home is a bathtub with a slippery surface. The best way to prevent bathtub falls is to install nonskid rubber decals. They will not only improve the safety of the tub but, when placed over chips or other minor imperfections, will enhance its appearance as well. A clear nonskid material, which is virtually unnoticeable other than its texture, is good news for people who don't like floral or other patterns in the bottom of the tub. For the decals to adhere, the surface of the tub must be clean and dry. Use a household cleaner designed to remove oil and soap scum and a nylon brush or dish-scrubbing pad.

A simple grab bar can make getting into and out of the tub less of a chore, particularly for the old and very young. Made of chrome, plated brass, brass, or brushed nickel, grab bars are mounted directly onto the wall surface. It is important that these fixtures be anchored into the wall studs and not just attached to the wallboard or tile. For example, if the bathroom wall is tile, use a masonry bit to drill through the tile, and screw the grab bar to the wall stud behind it.

A sudden rush of hot water while you are showering can be merely annoying, or it can be dangerous. This commonly occurs with nonmixing, two-handled faucets when a nearby toilet is flushed or a sink is used, because these other fixtures reduce the amount of cold water flowing to the shower.

Antiscald or pressure-balanced shower valves are designed to deliver a steady stream of temperature-controlled water that is virtually unaffected by demands placed on the water in other areas of the house. These devices are not as easy to install as a lavatory faucet, but safety concerns make this upgrade well worth the effort.

Regrouting and Recaulking

Both regrouting and recaulking are ongoing preventive maintenance projects that can help you avoid larger, more costly projects in the future. Grout and caulk that are kept in good condition prevent water from seeping into cabinets, wallboard, wall framing, and subflooring. By the time damage of this sort is discovered, costly replacement of the affected areas is often the only solution.

Because ceramic tile has many joints, it requires more ongoing maintenance than other products manufactured as solid sheets. Most homeowners balk at the chore, but ceramic tile will look better and last longer if it is cleaned and regrouted at least annually. This is especially important if

the tile is installed directly over wallboard without the benefit of a mortar bed.

Grout is sold packaged as a dry powder in a variety of colors; it is available at most hardware stores and home-improvement centers. The first step in installing new grout is to remove about ⅛ inch of the existing grout with a hammer and chisel or the sharp-pointed end of an old-fashioned bottle opener. This will provide a depression for the new grout to occupy.

Next, mix the grout with water to form a paste, following the instructions on the package. Apply the grout with a rubber float or a sponge, forcing the grout into the joints in a diagonal direction. Wipe off excess grout immediately with a damp sponge. Any grout residue that remains on the tile will form a haze and can be polished off with a dry piece of cheesecloth. Wait a few days for the grout to dry completely, and then apply a coat of acrylic sealer to both the tile and the grout.

Important: Fill the joint between the tile and the bathtub or shower pan halfway with grout and then top it with a bead of clear silicone caulk. The caulk will provide flexibility at a joint where there is typically a considerable amount of movement.

Apply clear silicone caulk at all locations where cultured products or other solid-surface materials are joined or where they meet fixtures or other finishes. It is imperative that the surface be clean and completely dry before you install new

caulk, to minimize the possibility of future mildew growth behind it.

Caulk the joint between any vinyl floor covering and the tub or shower pan. Use a latex caulk with silicone, which is simple to install and will remain flexible. All the vulnerable locations in a bathroom can be recaulked in less than an hour at very little expense.

Eradicating Mildew

Mildew is a fungal growth that thrives in warm, dark, damp areas. It looks unappealing and has a strong odor. The key to long-term mildew control is to rid the area completely of dormant mildew spores and then to maintain proper ventilation and sufficient natural lighting to help avoid future growth of mildew.

One of the most effective deterrents to mildew is a solution of ⅓ cup laundry detergent, 1 quart laundry bleach, and 3 quarts warm water. Add the bleach to the water first, and then add the detergent. Even though the solution is mild, be sure to wear rubber gloves, eye protection, and old clothes. Also be sure that there is plenty of ventilation.

Apply the solution to affected areas with a sponge or nylon brush. Let the solution sit until all the dark stains have disappeared (about 15 minutes), but don't allow the solution to dry. Repeat the process a second time if needed.

Many medium upgrades can be precipitated by small upgrades; for example, you may want a new countertop after installing a new sink or faucet. Medium upgrades cost between $500 and $2,000 and can be completed in two to six days. Because of their complexity, they may require the services of a professional.

Adding a Cabinet

Most people agree that bathrooms never have enough storage space for towels, linens, toiletries, and assorted paraphernalia. This is especially true if you have a wall-hung or pedestal sink rather than a vanity.

Depending on the location of the new cabinet, this remodeling project may or may not require you to tear out anything. To install a vanity in place of a wall-hung or pedestal sink, it is necessary to remove the existing sink and start from scratch, incorporating a new countertop into your design. However, it is often possible to install a new cabinet in an out-of-the-way spot in the bathroom—behind a door, in an otherwise unusable corner, or over the toilet.

Most home-improvement centers, hardware stores, and lumberyards stock prefabricated cabinets in a variety of sizes designed to fit almost any need. For hard-to-fit spots, a cabinetmaker can offer alternative solutions.

Whether the cabinet is custom-made or prefabricated, there are several things to look for. The first is quality of construction and finish. Some very fine examples of cabinetry are produced by production manufacturers; others are only slightly better than a cardboard box.

Most American-made cabinet bodies (the sides, back, bottom, and shelves) are constructed of raw particleboard, laminated or veneered particleboard, or veneered plywood. All these materials are acceptable, provided they are substantial enough in size. Material for the sides, bottom, and shelves should be at least ¾ inch thick. In fine cabinets the face frames (the surface of the cabinet to which the doors are attached) are made from solid wood and are assembled with screws or dowels and glue.

The second thing to look at in a cabinet is the interior. Although most prefabricated cabinet bodies are prefinished, the interior is sometimes unfinished. Paint or varnish will not only enhance the interior of the cabinets, but will also eliminate the need to line them with shelf paper.

A popular finish for cabinet interiors is a heat-treated laminate called melamine—a smooth, uniform, permanent surface. Melamine-finished interiors will add slightly to the cost (about 10 percent) but are worth the expense in added convenience and cleanliness.

The final thing to look for in a cabinet is door style. Besides the finish, no other detail will have as much effect on the look of the cabinets. Solid raised-panel doors, due to their substantial construction, tend to be the most impressive in appearance and performance. They also add between 5 and 10 percent to the cost of the cabinets but are hard to beat in terms of lasting quality.

The cost of bathroom cabinets varies widely, depending on the cabinet size, construction, configuration, type of wood, and finish. Elaborate cabinets can fall outside the range of a small upgrade. Handy homeowners can use a how-to book on cabinetmaking and save hundreds of dollars. Just be sure that you don't create one problem in an attempt to solve another. Too many cabinets in too little space will not only be inconvenient to work around, but can make an already small bathroom look and feel even smaller.

Installing a Vanity

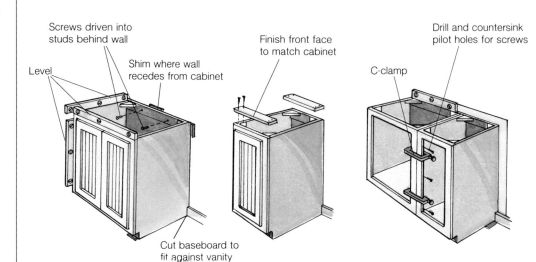

Screws driven into studs behind wall

Level

Shim where wall recedes from cabinet

Finish front face to match cabinet

Drill and countersink pilot holes for screws

C-clamp

Cut baseboard to fit against vanity

Use a level to check that cabinets are plumb and level in 3 directions

Set 2 × 4 frame on vanity to raise countertop height

Screw and glue cabinets together to extend vanity length

Bathroom Storage

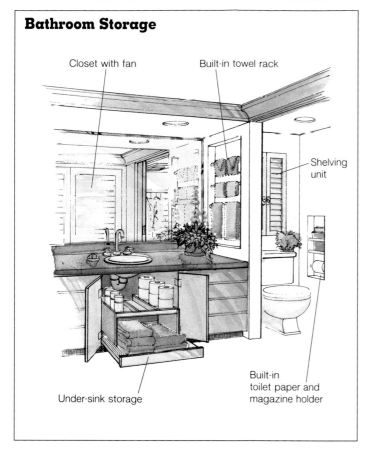

Closet with fan

Built-in towel rack

Shelving unit

Under-sink storage

Built-in toilet paper and magazine holder

Installing New Flooring

Because of the area it covers, flooring probably has as much to do with the appearance of a bathroom as any other finish. The most popular types of flooring include vinyl, ceramic tile, and carpet. Of the three, tile is probably the longest lasting. It is also the most costly to install, because a mortar bed should be laid down first. This not only adds to the integrity of the installation but makes for a smoother and more uniform finish that will better resist water.

If mortar or cementitious mortarboard is too costly or not available, consider something other than tile. Tile that is glued directly to a wood subfloor not only cannot be considered an upgrade but, due to the lack of thorough waterproofing, can actually diminish

the value of a house, no matter how good it may look at first. (This is not the case for all ceramic tile installed on the subfloor—only floors where moisture is a factor. For example, ceramic tile installed in an entry hall without mortar would be acceptable, provided that the floor framing was reinforced to minimize the amount of deflection. Deflection could result in cracked grout and loose or broken tile.)

Carpet is a good choice in a bathroom that is subject to minimal traffic and little or no water. Carpet may not be a good idea where there is a lot of traffic or water, especially in a bathroom used by small children, because it is not as easy to keep clean as a smooth, hard surface.

Typically, the installed cost of carpet and pad will be about one fifth the price of ceramic tile. Carpet installed in a bathroom that contains a tub or shower should have a waterproof membrane, such as vinyl, underneath to protect the wood floor below from leaks. This will add only slightly to the cost but will protect the floor from water damage.

Vinyl is probably the most popular of all bathroom floor coverings because of its moderate price and excellent wearability. Most of the cost of installing vinyl in a bathroom is labor. The material itself usually amounts to only about 25 percent of the total cost. No-wax vinyl is easy to maintain and comes in a huge selection of colors and patterns.

Installing Resilient Flooring

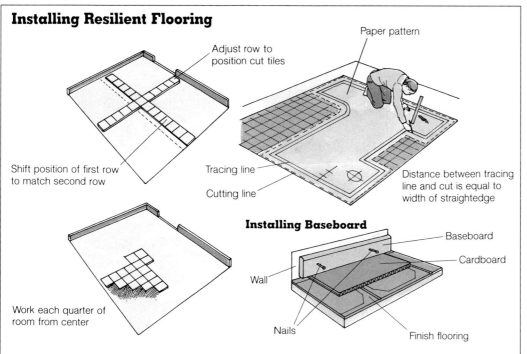

Adjust row to position cut tiles

Paper pattern

Shift position of first row to match second row

Tracing line

Cutting line

Distance between tracing line and cut is equal to width of straightedge

Work each quarter of room from center

Installing Baseboard

Baseboard

Cardboard

Wall

Nails

Finish flooring

Although vinyl can be installed over an existing layer of vinyl, most flooring experts recommend removing any existing floor covering. New underlayment should be installed over the wood subfloor to ensure a smooth and uniform surface for the new vinyl.

There are two basic ways to install sheet vinyl: laid flat with a baseboard or coved up the wall. Coved vinyl is more popular in a bathroom because it helps prevent water from traveling beyond the floor area under walls and cabinets, where repairs of water damage can be very expensive. You can minimize potential water damage with flat-laid vinyl by caulking the vinyl-to-baseboard joint with latex and silicone caulking (see page 65). Vinyl tiles don't hold up as well as sheet vinyl, although they are easier to install by the do-it-yourselfer. If you use vinyl tiles, avoid the preglued type.

Installing a New Countertop

A new countertop can have a dramatic effect on a bathroom, offering a fresh and interesting surface. A new countertop need not match the existing form, style, or finish, and it can be any shape and size. It can even be extended over the back of the toilet to create a more streamlined look and additional counter space.

If the new countertop is a cultured or solid-surface material, such as cultured onyx, cultured marble, or Corian®, the basin and countertop can be constructed in one piece. This

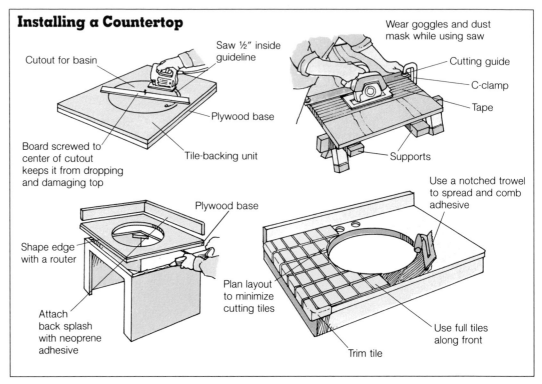

Installing a Countertop

Cutout for basin

Saw ½" inside guideline

Plywood base

Board screwed to center of cutout keeps it from dropping and damaging top

Tile-backing unit

Wear goggles and dust mask while using saw

Cutting guide

C-clamp

Tape

Supports

Plywood base

Shape edge with a router

Attach back splash with neoprene adhesive

Plan layout to minimize cutting tiles

Use a notched trowel to spread and comb adhesive

Trim tile

Use full tiles along front

seamless configuration eliminates the need for caulking or grouting. It also greatly simplifies installation.

If you prefer a basin that is separate from the countertop, the choices are ceramic tile, plastic laminate, marble, granite, and cultured or solid-surface material. Ceramic tile, marble, and granite are the most costly finishes. Unless you are skilled, have the installation done by a professional. Ceramic tile should be installed in mortar on a wood substrate. Although it requires occasional regrouting, it is one of the most durable finishes, resisting scratching and staining significantly better than cultured or other synthetic solid-surface materials. (See also pages 47 and 53.)

Installing a Garden Window

A garden window lets you enjoy the outdoors and have privacy at the same time: The outdoors is still clearly visible, but the ability to see in is obscured by the greenery. A garden window can also be a welcome space saver when valuable bathroom counter space is currently occupied by houseplants.

One of the most attractive aspects of this project is the ease with which it can be accomplished. The most cost-effective way to install a garden window is to remove the existing window and replace it with one of a matching size; no framing changes will be required, and the amount of interior and exterior patching will be minimal. To maintain the

harmony of both the interior and exterior, the garden window should be finished to match the other windows in the house.

Prices for garden windows vary widely according to size and style. Although this project is considered a medium upgrade, it can be completed in a day.

Adding an Exhaust Fan

An exhaust fan is one of the best ways to avoid the buildup of moisture and mildew in a bathroom and hence the damage that often follows. A fan should be used in addition to any ventilation provided by an openable window, because a window will not move the volume of air that a properly sized fan will move, and it is frequently not opened during cold weather.

Exhaust fans are rated according to the cubic feet of air moved per minute (cfm). To determine the minimum cfm required for a bathroom fan, multiply the length of the bathroom by its width, and then multiply that number by 1.1. For example, a 5-foot by 9-foot room has 45 square feet; $45 \times 1.1 = 49.5$, for a minimum of a 50-cfm exhaust fan.

In addition to the basic exhaust fan, some fans come complete with lights and fan-forced radiant heaters that will make any bathroom more comfortable to use. A heat-fan-light combination can pay for itself in less than a year, based on the amount of energy that is saved in heating the entire home just to get the bathroom warm enough for showering on cold winter mornings.

Because installing an exhaust fan has become such a popular do-it-yourself project, many of these products are packed with nontechnical installation instructions and even have toll-free consumer hotlines.

Exhaust fans, fan-light combinations, and heat-fan-light combinations are installed in basically the same way, with the two latter units requiring a little more electrical work.

For the most efficient movement of air, attach the fan housing to the framing at the highest point in the ceiling. All fans should be ducted to the exterior, not into the attic, via a flexible aluminum or plastic tube that originates at the fan housing and terminates at a roof jack or termination cap attached to the roof. Attach this tubing at both ends with two sheet metal screws. Also, wrap the connections with duct tape to ensure a virtually airtight fit.

Although you do not need to install a basic exhaust fan or a fan-light combination on a separate electrical circuit, building codes require that most heat-fan or heat-fan-light combinations be installed on a separate circuit. Also consider placing the different functions on separate switches for more flexibility and less energy consumption.

Because installing an exhaust fan involves electrical and mechanical work, check with local building officials to see if a permit is required.

The modest use of marble kept remodeling costs in this bathroom to a minimum—small marble squares highlight a limestone floor, with marble cabinet handles and drawer pulls and a thin inlay of green marble on the shower wall to continue the theme. The curved glass of the shower cost less than a sliding glass shower door and echoes the curves used throughout the house, also seen on pages 1 and 45.

LARGE BATHROOM UPGRADES

Large upgrades cost more than $2,000, although some can be completed in a day or two. Enlarging a bathroom generally takes at least a week, whereas adding a showerhead to an existing tub can take just a few days and cause a minimum of disruption. A project categorized as large doesn't necessarily mean a large disruption.

Adding a Showerhead to an Existing Tub

The addition of a showerhead will significantly improve the usefulness of an existing tub and of the bathroom in general. In new homes it is rare to find a tub without a showerhead, unless there is a separate stall shower in the same room.

Although not having a showerhead probably isn't a problem as long as the primary users of the bathroom containing the tub are small children, keep in mind that before long they too will want the convenience of a shower.

A successful installation depends on finishing several tasks before adding the showerhead. First, remove the existing tub valve and replace it with a new combination tub and shower valve that will allow the user to select one or the other. You will need to turn off the water supply to the house while changing the valve. It's a good idea to let everyone in the house know when this is to take place so that they will be able to plan their activities that require water.

You will have to remove the wallcovering surrounding the existing valve in order to extract the valve. No special care need be given to the wallcovering surrounding the tub, since it will have to be replaced with a waterproof surface.

Once you have removed the existing valve, install the new valve according to the manufacturer's directions. If the old valve was installed with galvanized pipe and the new valve is to be installed with copper pipe, be sure to use dielectric unions that will keep the dissimilar metals from deteriorating via electrolytic action.

Before cutting the vertical length of pipe that will run from the valve to the showerhead, hold the new showerhead up to the framing to determine a height that will be suitable for those using the shower. Make a pencil mark on the framing, and measure from it to the valve to determine the length of pipe that will be required. The average showerhead is about 6 feet above the floor.

Once you have roughed in the new valve and showerhead, expose the wall framing by removing the balance of the wallcovering that surrounds the tub, from the top ledge of the tub to the ceiling. This will allow you to inspect and repair any water or fungus damage to the wood framing members surrounding the tub. Consult a contractor

authorized to diagnose and make repairs if you suspect even the slightest damage.

Apply a vapor barrier over the framing, followed by a layer of water-resistant wallboard, mortarboard, or a bed of mortar, depending on the wallcovering that you will use. Water-resistant wallboard is an excellent substrate for solid-surface material, such as cultured marble, cultured onyx, or Corian®. Mortarboard or a mortar bed is a must if the wallcovering will be ceramic tile or marble tile. Although the new wallcovering can go to the ceiling, it is especially important that it extend at least 6 inches above the showerhead, usually 6½ feet above the floor.

Finally, install a new tub enclosure or a curtain and rod

to protect the surrounding area from water damage. Do not install a new tub enclosure until the surrounding wallcovering has had a chance to set, typically not less than 48 hours. Furthermore, allow the caulk that surrounds the frame of the new enclosure to dry for a minimum of 24 hours before using the shower. This will help to ensure a watertight seal. (See Replacing a Tub Enclosure on page 61 for more information.)

The cost of this improvement will vary according to the size and height of the tub enclosure and the type of wallcovering selected. Cultured marble and cultured onyx are among the most popular materials, and they are also the least costly because no mortar bed is needed under the product, which saves on labor.

Adding a Showerhead

- Eared elbow attached to blocking
- 2-by blocking
- 2 × 4 stud
- Shower riser
- Tub valve assembly
- Hot-water supply
- Cold-water supply
- Spout 4" above top of tub
- Replace old spout with new diverter spout
- Stub-out for showerhead 66"–78"
- Tub valve assembly 26"–36"

These materials are also among the most versatile in terms of design. Both come in a wide range of colors and patterns, offering almost limitless decorating possibilities.

Corian® is another popular but expensive solid-surface material. It is seamless and is installed in much the same way as cultured products. Unlike cultured products, however, Corian® has no surface finish that can separate from the core; it is of a uniform substance throughout. The manufacturer recommends polishing the surface of the product with a dish-scrubbing pad to maintain a clean and attractive finish.

Ceramic tile is the most versatile material in terms of color, size, shape, texture, and finish. Ceramic tile installed in mortar is second only to Corian® and other solid-surface materials as far as cost is concerned. Unique and interesting patterns and designs can be created with ceramic tile—an effect that can't be achieved with other materials. The main disadvantage to ceramic tile is the ongoing maintenance associated with the grout that surrounds each tile (see page 65). Corian® with a decorative border is a popular alternative that almost eliminates the grout maintenance necessary with a horizontal ceramic tile installation.

Marble tile has become one of the most popular upscale bathroom wallcoverings. The natural veining and patterns that are inherent to marble add unusual interest and elegance to any bathroom. However, because of the depth and density of the patterns, marble tile can be overwhelming in small spaces. An advantage to marble

tile is that because of the large size of individual tiles (usually 12 inches square), there are fewer grout joints than with standard-sized ceramic tile, and the joints are significantly narrower, making maintenance considerably easier.

Installing a Skylight

A skylight can convert a dark, uninviting bathroom into a light and cheerful space. It is especially useful in a bathroom without a window or an exterior wall where a window could be installed. Unfortunately, many roof-framing configurations prohibit the installation of a skylight. A thorough inspection of the roof in the attic will determine whether you can install a skylight.

A skylight adds architectural interest to the bathroom, and an operable unit greatly enhances ventilation. Skylights are sold with hand cranks or automatic openers. Other popular options include tinted glass, energy-saving gas-filled thermal glazing, and retractable shades.

Because the installation of a skylight typically involves carpentry work, wallboard, insulation, roofing, sheet metal, and painting, this project is often best performed by a professional. A home-improvement or remodeling contractor is most likely to be able to help you. According to statistics gathered by major construction and real estate organizations, the addition of a skylight offers one of the best returns on the investment. For more information see page 54.

Enlarging the Bathroom

When you need more space for a bathroom remodeling project—for a second sink, a separate shower, a bidet, a whirlpool tub, or added storage space—the major decision is where to obtain the added space. You can take space from an adjoining room, eliminating a closet or reducing the size of the adjoining room itself, for example.

A project of this magnitude requires a well-thought-out bathroom design as well as attention to the impact on the adjoining room. If it is a bedroom, will the smaller room still be comfortable and accommodate your furniture? Would taking over the entire adjoining bedroom be more appropriate? This is especially popular in homes with four or more

bedrooms that have two or fewer bathrooms and where the master bedroom and bathroom are both too small. In such cases, the existing master bedroom, master bathroom, and an adjoining bedroom can be combined to create a new master bedroom suite that includes one large bedroom with perhaps a sitting area, increased closet space, and a larger, more elaborate bathroom.

As you can see, what begins as the need for a second sink or a tub separate from the shower can balloon into something considerably more complex. The project can be very expensive if the new design calls for moving the plumbing fixtures, especially if there is no crawl space and the floor consists of a slab on grade. Other structural concerns may further complicate the project.

Skylights, neutral vinyl flooring, a sit-down vanity, and brass fixtures and drawer pulls exhibit a range of upgrades that can add distinction to a bathroom without undue expense.

Because of the complexity of this upgrade, in terms of both design and construction, it is generally a good idea to enlist the services of a design-and-build contractor, a designer or space planner, or an architect. In addition to helping create a workable design solution, the person you choose will also be able to point out any potential design or construction pitfalls that should be addressed.

The proposed plan should be presented to local building officials to ensure that it meets current health, building, and safety codes. A building permit will most likely be necessary before construction begins. Periodic inspections will be required during the construction of the project.

Because a project such as this can range in cost from $5,000 to more than $50,000, you should give a great deal of consideration to the budget as well as the design.

Adding a Whirlpool Tub

A whirlpool tub can turn even the simplest bathroom into a more pleasant place to be. Aside from the added comfort that these tubs offer, they enhance the overall look of the bathroom. Whirlpool tubs are sold in a variety of shapes, sizes, materials, colors, and finishes.

Like other bathtubs, whirlpools are available in enameled steel, cast iron, cultured marble or onyx, acrylic, and teak. They can also be custom-built in place with tile, granite, or marble. The prefabricated models are available with a skirted front similar to that of conventional

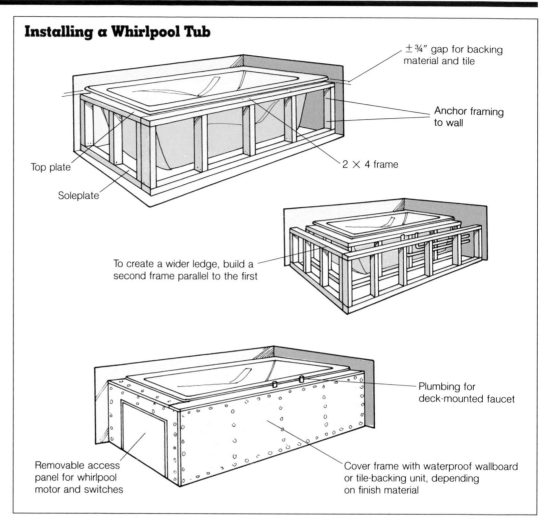

Installing a Whirlpool Tub

± ¾" gap for backing material and tile

Anchor framing to wall

2 × 4 frame

Top plate

Soleplate

To create a wider ledge, build a second frame parallel to the first

Plumbing for deck-mounted faucet

Removable access panel for whirlpool motor and switches

Cover frame with waterproof wallboard or tile-backing unit, depending on finish material

tubs or in self-rimming styles, which are designed to rest on platforms. The platforms are constructed of wood and then finished with the same type of material used to surround the tub.

Decorative ledges and interesting designs are possible with either type of tub. The skirt is sometimes removable to provide access to the pump motor. Building codes require that there be access to this motor; this can be achieved via an exterior access or through an adjoining closet or room, should the configuration allow.

Enameled cast-iron tubs are usually the most expensive, not only for the tub itself but for labor and installation materials, which can cost almost as much as the tub, depending on the changes that are required to install the tub and the type of wallcovering you choose to surround it. Acrylic tubs are the most popular and offer the greatest selection of shapes and sizes. They cost about two thirds as much as enameled cast-iron tubs and are considered easier to install.

The size of the pump motor and the number of jets will also greatly influence the cost of the tub. Most tubs are equipped with either a ¾-horsepower or a 1-horsepower motor and from four to six jets. Additional jets are available; in some cases you can specify the location of the jets if the tub is a special order. For example, if the lower back or feet would benefit most from the jets, the tub can be configured that way.

The most cost-effective way to add a whirlpool tub is to replace the existing tub with one of the same size, although this may be difficult if the existing tub is the standard 60 inches by 30 inches. Most whirlpool tubs are larger and more elaborate than standard tubs and are frequently large enough to accommodate more than one person. However, an aggressive search will probably reveal a variety of tubs that will work within the confines of the existing space.

If you would like a more spacious tub, some minor framing changes may be all that is required for installation. For example, you may find a tub that matches the existing tub in length but is a little wider (36 to 42 inches), which would greatly enhance the comfort of the tub and even provide space for more than one person to enjoy at a time. However, avoid installing a tub so large that it overwhelms the space or makes using the other areas of the bathroom either unsafe or uncomfortable.

Installing a new whirlpool tub involves many different aspects of construction. For example, it will be necessary to remove the wallcovering and wallboard surrounding the existing tub to make way for the installation of the new tub and surround. If the new tub will not have a showerhead, the new surround can be as simple as a 12-inch splash to protect the wallboard surrounding the tub. If the tub will have a showerhead, the wallcovering should be waterproof (tile, for example) and will need to extend at least 6 inches above the showerhead.

Once the wallcovering, wallboard, and existing tub have been removed, make any framing changes needed to accommodate the new tub. Plumbing and electrical changes can be made at this time also. It's likely that you will need to relocate and perhaps replace the tub faucet.

There may be space on the deck of the new tub for a deck-mounted tub filler instead of a conventional faucet. Many new bathtubs include filler valves that are installed as a part of the tub. Underwater light kits are also available, but keep in mind that these elaborate options combined can cost as much as the base price of the tub.

In addition to the plumbing work required to reconfigure the water supply, the drain and waste system will most likely need to be reworked as well. More often than not the existing drain will need to be altered to accept the waste from the new tub. The final bit of plumbing work will involve installing the pump motor. Although most of the tubs manufactured today are preplumbed, with all jets and pipes assembled, some minor connections will still need to be made on site.

Due to the size of the pump motor, a separate electrical circuit will be required with at least a 20-amp breaker and a 15-amp ground fault circuit interrupter (GFCI). This means running the electrical wire from a new circuit breaker at the subpanel to the new pump. The electrical connection at the pump motor is typically concealed under the tub. You can have an optional timer switch installed to limit the amount of time that the whirlpool function is used and to control the motor speed. Many tubs offer an optional air switch that allows you fingertip control of the various functions of the tub and avoids your having to get out of the tub to operate the timer. These safe, handy devices are generally located right on the tub ledge and have become almost mandatory options.

Adding a Bathroom

Of all the improvements that can be made to a home, the addition of a bathroom not only lends the most favorable return on the dollar invested but has a dramatically positive effect on the family's life-style, especially in a home with too many people and too few bathrooms.

Is an addition to the home necessary, or can the new bathroom be located within the existing floor area? In either case, where will it be located? How large will the new bathroom be, and what facilities will it include? These are just a few of the many questions that you will need to address when considering a bathroom addition.

The best place to start is by making a list of what should be included in the bathroom. Will there be a tub, a shower, or both? Is one sink adequate, or is there a need for two? Is a window important, or will a skylight suffice? The answers to these and other questions will help to determine the amount of space required and the approximate cost. This will in turn help to determine whether you can include this upgrade within existing living space or if an addition will be required.

Decorating magazines, home-improvement books, and model homes will give you ideas on how the space might work. Look into classes that the local community college may offer and how-to seminars offered by trade organizations. Home-improvement and home and garden shows are also good sources of ideas and information. Homeowners can examine a variety of products in the presence of a representative who can answer specific questions. Often, experts on home improvement are available to discuss a project in general, from planning through construction.

You can seek additional design and planning assistance from an architect, designer or space planner, or a designer and builder. Sometimes you will need input from a combination of these professionals. The fee for the design should be between 5 and 10 percent of the projected cost of the improvement. An additional 3 to 5 percent is added to the base design fee if the person will select materials and supervise the project.

Before planning a bathroom addition, give serious consideration to the amount of money you can budget for the project, which will likely influence your decisions about many of the design considerations just discussed.

A bathroom remodeling project is as complex to build as it is to design. Unless you are unusually handy, have an open-ended schedule, or are willing to take time off from work, you will need to have a general contractor perform the work.

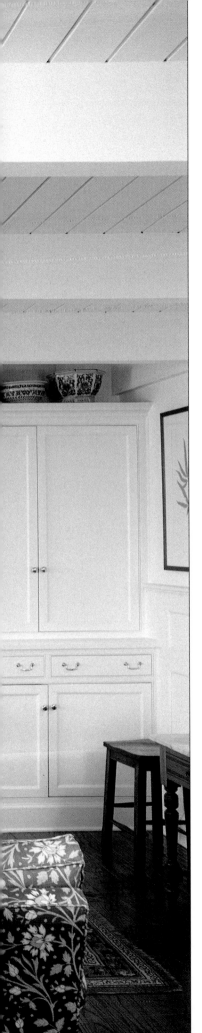

LIVING AREAS

Many improvements made to living areas are decorative and involve a light touch, such as rearranging the furniture or installing new window coverings. However, these changes are not permanent, so they are not technically considered home improvements. The upgrades discussed in this chapter include improvements that will be built into the home and will remain with it even if it is sold. Examples include wainscoting, chair rail, lighting, windows, doors, decorative wood moldings, and a wet bar.

Although many of these upgrades can be completed by the average do-it-yourselfer, you might want to enlist the support of a decorator or an interior designer to look at your home and make suggestions about the projects you have in mind.

Many of these projects reflect personal taste. You should carefully consider any project that is so owner specific that it will not appeal to a future buyer and may actually have to be removed or altered when you sell the house. Advice from an interior designer or a realtor can be helpful when you are considering such changes.

Fireplace refacing and a period mantel, found in a salvage yard, are the focal points of this living room. A built-in home entertainment center hides the television and other electronics.

SMALL LIVING-AREA UPGRADES

Replacing outdated lighting and revealing hardwood floors under old carpeting are small upgrades that can dramatically transform a living room or family room. For homeowners with a limited remodeling budget, this can be the place to begin. These small upgrades cost less than $500 and can be completed in a day or two.

Refinishing Hardwood Floors

Owners of many homes built before the 1970s may be pleased and surprised to find hardwood flooring in pristine condition buried beneath layers of shag carpeting and pads. You might consider it literally a buried treasure, because hardwood flooring is now one of the most popular floor finishes, in spite of its expense to install new. It lends elegance to a room, and with proper maintenance it will last far longer than most other flooring, including carpet, vinyl, and tile.

If you suspect that hardwood flooring lies beneath old wall-to-wall carpet, pull up a small section of carpet and the underlying pad at one corner of a room. If a hardwood floor does exist, pull up all the carpet and pad; this is the only way to evaluate the condition of the entire floor. If there are no serious stains, you can probably restore the floor to its original condition after replacing any damaged boards.

An older floor may not need refinishing if it is merely dulled by several layers of old wax and grime. To see if this is the case, rub a small area with steel wool dipped in alcohol until you have removed all layers of wax. Then damp-mop the bare wood and apply paste wax. If this brings satisfactory results, clean the entire floor.

An unsightly stain usually cannot be removed, but you may be able to bleach it to minimize its impact, or you can cover it with furniture or a rug.

Living-Area Upgrades

For an overview of the dining room and living room, before and after remodeling, see pages 6 and 7.

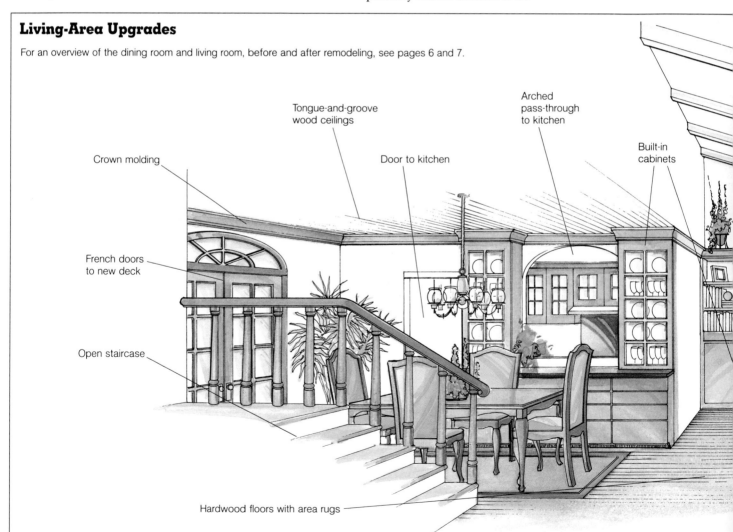

Crown molding

Tongue-and-groove wood ceilings

Door to kitchen

Arched pass-through to kitchen

Built-in cabinets

French doors to new deck

Open staircase

Hardwood floors with area rugs

If the floor is riddled with staples used to install the carpet and pad or is worn severely or stained unevenly, you will need to sand and refinish the floor. This will involve renting a drum sander and edger (a rotary sander). These tools require practice and strength to operate. Used improperly they will scar the floor.

If you choose to sand the floor yourself, get complete instructions before you begin, and practice in a back room or closet. After thoroughly sanding and vacuuming the floor, seal the floor with either a clear floor sealer or a stain. Once dry,

apply at least two coats of floor finish, such as polyurethane, following the manufacturer's directions. The entire process of sanding and refinishing will take from three to five days, depending on drying times and the number of rooms. But the payoff in beauty, maintenance, and durability makes it worth the inconvenience.

Replacing Old Lighting

The replacement of old light fixtures is often overlooked as an easy, inexpensive, effective

way to add style, function, and importance to any room. Whereas installing new light fixtures (see page 88) involves new wiring, replacing outdated fixtures is easily done by the do-it-yourselfer.

Consider the following when selecting replacement fixtures.

☐ Style. The fixture should coordinate with your other furnishings to create a pulled-together look: Modern lighting looks best with contemporary furniture, classic lighting with period furniture.

☐ Size. A fixture that is too large can overpower a room,

and one that is too small may not provide enough of a statement, not to mention inadequate lighting.

☐ Weight. If the fixture weighs more than 50 pounds, as some chandeliers do, the electrical box must be attached directly to a joist or other framing.

☐ Mounting hardware. If the old fixture doesn't have a standard electrical ceiling box, you will have to install one.

☐ Ground wire. The electrical box for fixtures with metal parts, including swag lights, must be grounded even if the old box was not.

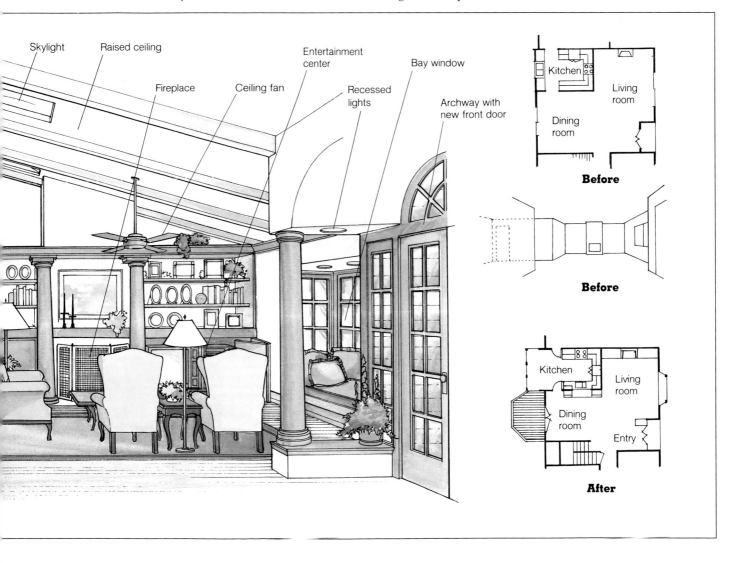

Installing Recessed Lighting

A series of recessed fixtures installed at the edge of the ceiling close to a wall and equipped with wall-wash reflectors will cast a waterfall of light that can liven up an otherwise undramatic space. Wall-wash trim can be added to a fixture to highlight a specific object, such as a painting. Recessed downlights can highlight an area of a room, light a game table, or provide reading light for a favorite chair. Recessed downlights also are a popular alternative to a dining room chandelier. Adjustable spot lighting or eyeball trim can also highlight a specific area.

Consider separate switching if you are planning to install two or more recessed light fixtures. This will allow for more versatility and can be more energy efficient as well. Dimmer switches are an added feature that will enhance the energy efficiency and overall appeal of this type of lighting (see page 38).

Painting

A fresh coat of paint can improve the appearance of a living room more than any other upgrade of similar cost. This homeowner-friendly task can usually be completed in a weekend.

When selecting paint, choose a light color and avoid trendy colors, which can soon look outdated. Dark colors tend to make an already small room appear even more cramped. Light colors will make the space seem larger and more airy and will enhance natural light by reflecting it off of the walls and ceiling.

Flat latex paint is the most popular type of paint for areas of the home that are not exposed to constant moisture. Doors and woodwork are usually painted with an enamel, which is available in both oil-based and latex and is sold in a variety of lusters, ranging from a matte finish to a high-gloss finish.

Remove light fixtures, switch-plate covers, and electrical plug covers before beginning to paint. This is an opportune time to soak the covers in a solution of 1 cup ammonia and 1 gallon warm water. Otherwise, they may look dirty against the freshly painted walls. Cover the remaining light switches and electrical plugs with a 2-inch-wide strip of masking tape to keep them free of paint. This is also a good time to replace outdated doorknobs (see page 88).

Fill all nicks and scratches in the woodwork with wood putty or vinyl patching compound. Next, thoroughly dust the walls and ceiling, wash the surfaces with a strong household cleaner or trisodium phosphate (TSP) applied according to the manufacturer's directions. Finally, patch and sand any holes or damaged areas in the walls and ceiling, using a vinyl patching compound or similar patching product, before you start to paint.

Installing a Ceiling Fan

Decorative ceiling fans and light-fan combinations suggest a luxurious yet casual life-style. These fixtures are attractive and energy efficient, especially in rooms with high ceilings. Ceiling fans with reversible motors can provide a breeze in summer and draw warm air down from the ceiling in winter. Because they circulate the air in the room, they help to minimize condensation build-up on the inside of windows and skylights. They are available in a wide variety of styles and finishes appropriate to modern settings or elaborate traditional settings, in living rooms, family rooms, and dining rooms, even in bedrooms. Some fixtures will lend a formal look; others will give the space a casual, airy feeling. For longevity and quiet operation select one that has a clutch and is properly balanced.

Additional ceiling framing or blocking may be necessary to adequately carry the weight of the new fixture. If more than routine electrical work is required to install the fan, consult an electrician or a how-to book on electrical wiring before proceeding.

Adding a Dimmer Switch

Lighting is a major design element in any room, and a simple way to make a dramatic change is by replacing a conventional toggle switch with a dimmer switch. Dimmers are most effective for dining room and living room lights and in family rooms where television viewing is a major activity. Be sure that you are replacing a two-way (single-pole) or three-way switch with the same type of dimmer (see page 38).

The switch, which can be installed in about 15 minutes, improves the versatility of an existing light fixture by allowing you to choose when you want bright light and when you want to create a special mood. By using one dimmer switch to control overhead lights and another to control accent lights, you can transform any room from a bright work space to a room for quiet contemplation.

Adding a Pass-Through

Passing food and utensils between the kitchen and an adjacent dining room is easy with a pass-through, which is simply an opening in the wall common to the two rooms, usually at counter height. This popular feature offers an excellent return on investment both in terms of convenience and dollar value.

Once you have cut the opening, simply wrap the pass-through with wallboard and cover it to match the existing wallcovering or, for a more finished look, trim it with decorative molding. You can add bifold louvered doors to help separate the two spaces, allowing the kitchen to be seen only when the doors are open. Paint or stain the trim and doors to match the other trim in the house.

A pass-through is an improvement that most homeowners can complete in a day or two without professional help. Locate the opening where it is convenient to both spaces and where it will not interfere with existing or planned furnishings on the wall.

Note: If the only place to locate the pass-through contains plumbing and or electrical

Building an Arched Pass-Through

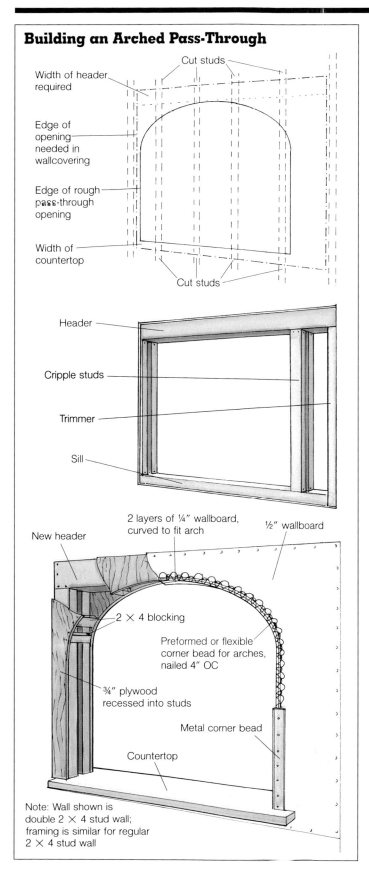

Width of header required

Cut studs

Edge of opening needed in wallcovering

Edge of rough pass-through opening

Width of countertop

Cut studs

Header

Cripple studs

Trimmer

Sill

2 layers of ¼" wallboard, curved to fit arch

½" wallboard

New header

2 × 4 blocking

Preformed or flexible corner bead for arches, nailed 4" OC

¾" plywood recessed into studs

Metal corner bead

Countertop

Note: Wall shown is double 2 × 4 stud wall; framing is similar for regular 2 × 4 stud wall

---

wiring, the work required to relocate these items will qualify this as a medium upgrade.

Installing Wainscoting or Chair Rail

Wainscoting capped with chair rail and either painted or left natural can enhance a simple dining room. You can even use chair rail alone. To add elegance, paper the wall above the chair rail and install crown molding at the ceiling.

Wainscoting made from oak or ash with a natural hand-rubbed or clear varnished finish is best in a small room, since a dark stain can make a small room look smaller and a dark room look darker. Paint is another option, either in a light color to complement the other finishes in the room or in a color that is coordinated with a contrasting paint or wallpaper on the wall above the wainscoting.

Wainscoting made of knotty pine with a pickled finish is an attractive addition to a kitchen or family room but may be too informal for a living room or dining room. Painted wood wainscoting, on the other hand, is attractive in any room of the house.

Traditional wainscoting is constructed of individual boards in a tongue-and-groove format that is trimmed with chair rail molding along the top and baseboard molding along the bottom. An easier method is to use sheets of plywood instead of individual boards, trimmed in the same way. Installing plywood is much easier, because individual boards

require a row of horizontal blocking between the studs. The plywood can simply be glued on top of the wallcovering with paneling adhesive and nailed at each stud.

You can construct wood wainscoting by cutting down full sheets of veneer paneling, or you can cut tongue-and-groove material to fit. Major home-improvement centers and hardware stores carry precut and packaged material.

Adding a Mantel

In some contemporary homes, there is no mantel above the fireplace. Because some homeowners prefer the uniform, uninterrupted look of a floor-to-ceiling fireplace facade, the cost-effectiveness of adding a mantel is not as great as some of the more universally accepted projects in this chapter. However, homeowners who prefer a traditional look and who desire a place to display an old family clock or other memorabilia and hang Christmas stockings will value this upgrade as a source of family pleasure and a means of achieving a finished look on the fireplace wall.

A mantel should fit the theme of the home. For example, a timber mantel would be appropriate in a large family room featuring a large fireplace with a stone face from hearth to ceiling. A classic painted-wood mantel and fireplace surround would enhance a simple red-brick fireplace in a living room with period furniture.

A mantel can be constructed from stone, wood, or a wood frame covered with plaster. The fireplace opening must be surrounded by noncombustible surfaces, such as stone, tile, marble, or stucco (plain wallboard is not enough), that extend at least 12 inches above and to the sides of the fireplace opening. The hearth must extend at least 16 inches in front and 8 inches to each side of the fireplace opening; if the fireplace opening is 6 square feet or larger, the hearth must extend at least 20 inches in front and 12 inches to each side.

The mantel should be securely anchored and installed to meet local safety codes, which typically require metal supports spaced between 24 and 36 inches apart. Before proceeding with the installation, check with local building officials for the acceptable installation configuration.

Replacing Door and Window Casings and Baseboards

Wide door and window casings (trim) and baseboards lend a feeling of elegance and quality to a home and can be a cost-effective improvement in any home regardless of price range. Wide casings are found in expensive construction and were commonplace in most houses when construction materials and labor were less expensive than they are today. If your house has narrow trim and baseboards, this upgrade is for you.

The most cost-effective trim changes are those that are made to the entire house—not just to a door or two. Door and window trim that doesn't match throughout the house can look like an incomplete project rather than an upgrade. Although combining multiple

styles and trim finishes can be effective, it is best left to interior decorators and professional designers.

A special technique to remember when removing painted door and window trim is to use a sharp utility knife to score the connections where the trim meets both the jamb and the wall. This is important because the trim is usually sealed to the frame and the wall with caulk and paint, which combine to make an almost inseparable joint. Scoring reduces the possibility of damage to the wall and the frame.

Once you have pried away the old trim, nail the new, wider trim in place and caulk and then paint it. Bright finish nails (8 penny) are best for this job. When replacing trim it is wise to reinstall it with the same reveal at the frame as the original trim had.

Paint-grade trim is far easier and cheaper to install than stain-grade trim. With stain-grade trim, heavy caulk cannot be used in joints, so a considerable amount of planing, chiseling, and sanding is required to achieve a proper fit. Also a stained finish should be applied over a solid, single piece of wood; when the trim will be painted, you can use finger-joint stock (it is made of scrap wood whose joints look like interlocking fingers).

Adding Crown Molding

Crown molding—the sculptured trim used where the walls meet the ceiling—adds elegance to a room. This upgrade will look more appropriate and

will provide a good return on investment in homes in expensive neighborhoods. A two-bedroom, one-bath home in a modest neighborhood would not be an appropriate candidate for this upgrade.

Unlike door and window trim, crown molding does not have to be used in every room; however, it is sometimes wise to trim all the rooms that are in close proximity to one another. For example, when both the living room and dining room can be viewed from the entry, all three areas should have crown molding.

Crown molding looks best in rooms with at least 8-foot ceilings. Large rooms with high ceilings look best trimmed with wide crown molding. Select thinner trim for rooms with lower ceilings. In addition, crown molding should be reserved for flat ceilings; it should not be used on angled ones.

For a further discussion of crown molding and other decorative trim, see page 83.

Refinishing Wall Surfaces

Patching holes, filling cracks, and removing grease and dirt can make a home look fresh, clean, new, and in good repair. In homes that are 40 years old or more, consider these methods of wall refinishing as a part of the next scheduled paint job. A painted surface looks only as good as the wall beneath it— refinishing the wall is necessary to prepare for painting. Texturing can often hide these otherwise noticeable flaws.

Wall refinishing is usually less expensive than applying wallcovering. Refinishing walls will return five times the cost in homes 30 to 40 years old, and twice that in homes 40 to 60 years old.

Wainscoting, chair rail, crown molding, and small-paned windows are beautifully executed details that convey the sense of a period home.

Refacing a fireplace, adding an entertainment center, or replacing a full-height stairway wall with open stair rails are moderately priced upgrades that dramatically enhance a living area and provide a good return on investment. Medium upgrades cost from $500 to $2,000 and take from two to six days to complete.

Installing a Wood-Burning Stove

One of the reasons that wood-burning stoves are so popular with cost-conscious homeowners is the ease with which these energy-efficient devices can be installed. Whereas the addition of a fireplace requires the services of a professional and is considered a large upgrade, a handy do-it-yourselfer can install a wood-burning stove. This qualifies as a medium upgrade and offers a return on investment of between 150 and 200 percent. Naturally, professional installation will diminish the percentage return.

A real bonus is that these units are also considerably more heat efficient than conventional masonry fireplaces. And, if the wood-burning stove is placed in the center of a room, it will provide heat in all directions—a decided advantage over a fireplace.

A wood-burning stove requires a noncombustible finish, such as brick or stone, on the wall next to the stove as well as a hearth constructed from the same material. Once the stove is set in place, a metal flue pipe connects it to a metal chimney flashing on the roof.

Before purchasing a wood-burning stove, it is wise to check local ordinances, especially in cities, to see what the standards for wood-burning stove emissions are in your area.

Adding an Entertainment Center

An entertainment center—a built-in cabinet for a television, VCR, compact disc player, sound system, and related electronics—is handy in a room where the family usually gathers to relax. This unit can save floor space and can group essential but nondecorative furnishings in attractive cabinetry. Many entertainment centers consist of space behind glass doors for electronics, a cabinet with wood doors for a television, open shelving for books, and cabinet space for other essentials. This arrangement allows you to connect the television audio through the stereo sound system.

Due to the overwhelming popularity of home electronics and to the fact that most homes contain more than one type plus the associated essentials, an entertainment center offers a return of two to three times its cost.

Most built-in entertainment centers are custom made in a cabinet shop and can be designed and constructed to your specifications. Be sure to measure the height, depth, and width of all the items you'll want in the cabinet, allowing space for records, cassettes, and so forth. Units that hold more than a television, VCR, and stereo system may cost more than $2,000, ranking them as large upgrades.

Since an entertainment center is a sizable piece of furniture, it should be carefully located in the room. In a long family room, for example, locating the center on a short end wall would be more appealing than visually extending the length of the room by locating the center on a long wall.

Installing a Storage Cabinet

A storage cabinet can be of tremendous value in a storage-intensive room. In the dining room, a floor-to-ceiling storage cabinet can hold china, crystal, silverware, and linen. The cabinet can be constructed with both glass and solid doors, so that it can serve as a combination decorative china closet and functional storage cabinet. For a home short on closet space, portions of the cabinet can be lined with cedar to keep linens and woolens.

A storage cabinet in the living room or family room can hold games, photograph albums, photography equipment, and other items that need a safe, dry, and easily accessible location. With the addition of a fold-down front, a cabinet can double as a computer desk; all accessories are close at hand, and when the computer is not being used it's hidden behind cabinet doors.

You can have built-in storage cabinets constructed in a cabinet shop. Bring along a list or a sketch of the items you want to store in the cabinet, so that the cabinetmaker can create a design to suit your needs.

Refacing a Fireplace

Because a fireplace is often the showpiece of a room, an out-of-fashion or worn surface detracts from whatever other decorating has been done. Such a fireplace is a candidate for refacing—either removing the existing surface and replacing it or applying a new layer of stone, tile, or marble over the old surface. The latter is an option if the existing surface is structurally sound and can be made smooth and if the fireplace itself is sound. Have it inspected before you make any decisions.

An alternative to applying tile or marble directly to the old surface is to construct a wood frame around the existing facade, cover it with wallboard and then apply the tile, marble, or even plaster. This is a popular solution for homeowners who want a free-form look that incorporates graceful curves or unusual angles.

This is also a convenient time to consider the addition of a mantel (see page 79).

Because of the complexity of this project, it is advisable to seek the assistance of an interior designer or architect as well as a contractor.

Converting Stairway Walls to Open Stair Rails

Unless the stairwell and the room adjacent to it are quite large, stairway walls visually reduce the size of the room. The mind's eye tends to see a room as smaller than it is when partial walls keep one from viewing the full length of the room at a glance. Replacing solid stairway walls with open stair rails will give a feeling of space as well as add drama.

The easiest and the most cost-effective way to approach this upgrade is to cut off the wall diagonally at a point just above the stairway rather than cutting it off above each tread. This saves the cost of replacing the treads or tread-covering material, such as carpet or hardwood, which can be expensive. Further, stair rails mounted on top of the remaining portion of

the wall instead of stair to stair are less expensive to purchase and install.

Although the process of selecting, installing, and finishing open stair rails is too extensive to describe in this book, the following are a few important things to keep in mind when planning this

project. The stair posts will support the handrail (which will, in turn, hold the spindles) and must be firmly connected to the wall and floor framing. For example, a 3-foot-high post should extend down into the wall at least 2 feet and should be bolted to an adjacent stud with at least two ½-inch

through-bolts. The post at the lower end of the stairs should penetrate into the floor and be firmly bolted to framing members in the subarea. If a framing member is not close to the place where the post is located, cross-bracing should be installed and bolted to both the stair post and the floor framing.

Intrinsic value is added to this entry hall through attention to details, such as the trim that echoes the banister. The crown molding and door trim convey the sense of an older home.

L ARGE LIVING-AREA UPGRADES

Adding slope to a low ceiling, installing a fireplace, and adding a family room may require professional help, but a homeowner's sweat equity can save enough to pay for features that may otherwise not be affordable. Large upgrades cost more than $2,000, although some can be completed in a day or two.

Adding Slope to a Ceiling

Converting a flat ceiling to one that is sloped, or vaulted, can have a dramatic effect on the look and feel of a room. It can make a small room appear much larger.

A sloped ceiling also allows space to install shelves and ledges for plants and large decorative items, and it increases the wall space available to install windows for added light and ventilation. You can use tongue-and-groove material and open beams instead of wallboard for added richness.

This is a project best left to professionals. In fact, to determine whether your ceiling is a candidate for being sloped, and at what cost, it is best to consult an architect, an engineer, or a design-and-build contractor. Not all flat ceilings can be sloped cost-effectively, even if an attic does exist. You must consider existing framing and mechanical, plumbing, and electrical conditions, since relocating heat ducts, gas or water lines, and electrical wiring can add significantly to the cost of the project.

Adding Decorative Moldings

The traditional elegance inherent in decorative wood moldings adds charm and character to the living areas of a home, and can give a plain-looking room an air of quality and richness. With an enormous selection of prefabricated molding patterns available, the design possibilities are almost limitless. This improvement, best done by a professional, pays big dividends while you are living in the home as well as at resale.

Decorative wood moldings are an excellent way to highlight room features, such as a fireplace, an entertainment center, and other built-ins. You can combine prefabricated moldings to create a more elaborate built-up design.

For the best effect, paint or stain moldings to match the existing wood trim in a room. For example, if the existing window trim, doors, and baseboard are painted, any crown molding that you add should also be painted rather than stained. However, if you are striving for a natural oak look, you may want to install stained oak crown molding and then replace the other trim in the room with stained oak.

You can also cover the entire ceiling with wood, or you can add beams. Wood can be applied directly over the existing ceiling finish. Knotty pine, clear vertical-grain redwood, rough-sawn cedar, and oak are just a few of the most popular wood ceiling finishes. Although adding wood to a ceiling can impart a rich, earthy feeling, too much wood or too much dark-stained wood can make a room gloomy and uninviting. Beams are an alternative that add wood without overpowering a room. They can be solid or manufactured from veneered plywood or other wood solids.

Although it's hard to beat the quality of wood trim installed by an experienced finish carpenter, this is a project that many skilled do-it-yourselfers may wish to attempt, which would qualify it as a medium upgrade. Unlike other projects that must be finished quickly, such as remodeling a bathroom or kitchen, this project can be done at your leisure. For an inexperienced installer, time may be just what's required to do an above-average job.

Installing French Doors

French doors offer the natural beauty of wood and are a graceful alternative to a conventional aluminum sliding glass door. Furthermore, replacing a sliding glass door with two openable French doors doubles the ventilation in a room. As long as the size of the wall opening remains the same, you can accomplish this cost-effective upgrade in a weekend.

Most French doors are available in configurations of from 1 to 15 panes per door. The divisions are either true divided

Removing the wall between the living room and dining room adds light and spaciousness. The traditional tone is enhanced by the repetition of the ceiling trim on the windows, baseboard, and fireplace.

Skylight Shaft Variations

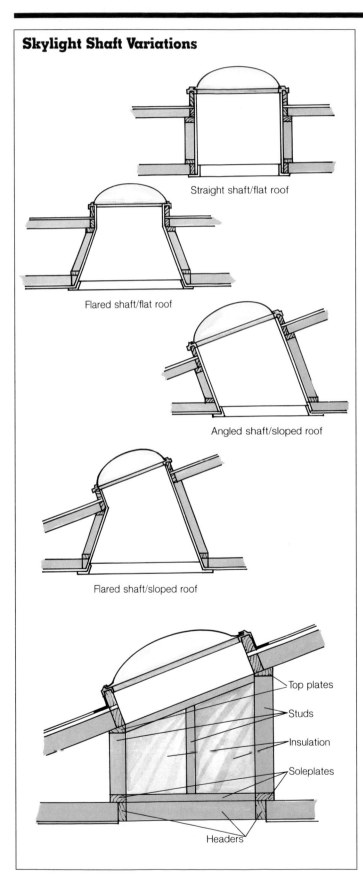

Straight shaft/flat roof

Flared shaft/flat roof

Angled shaft/sloped roof

Flared shaft/sloped roof

Top plates

Studs

Insulation

Soleplates

Headers

panes, with wood mullions (frames) surrounding each one, or they are a solid piece of glass with a wood grid applied to the interior surface to simulate individual panes.

Although wood is still the most popular finish for the interior of French doors, the exterior can be clad with vinyl or aluminum. Neither requires painting, and both are more weather-resistant than wood. For further information, see page 93.

Installing a Skylight

Skylights can make a dark, uninviting space look brighter and cheerier. Openable skylights can enhance ventilation, making a room more comfortable.

Locate a skylight in a part of the room that will most benefit from the added light, such as over a conversational grouping. If you must add a skylight off to one side, you may need a second skylight on the other side to balance it.

Skylights are complex to install and will generally require the expertise of a contractor. See pages 54 and 71 for further discussion.

Installing a Bay Window

Increased natural light, an enhanced view of the landscape, and added storage space are just a few of the benefits gained by installing a bay window. A bay window can give you the few extra inches you need to make dining room seating more comfortable when the table is extended.

The most common type of bay window is a 45-degree bay—a combination of three separate windows, with the side panels at a 45-degree angle to the center panel. The second most common type of bay window is a 30-degree bay.

The single greatest difference between the two types of windows is the distance that they project from the exterior of the structure. Given the same-sized opening, the 45-degree bay would project more than the 30-degree bay, an especially important detail when the new window is to be installed under the existing roof overhang.

Bay windows are sold with different roof styles, including copper roofs, shed roofs, hip roofs, and flat roofs. The roof design you choose should match the architecture of the rest of the house. For further information, see page 93.

Adding a Fireplace

One national remodeling association says that adding a fireplace to a home is the single most cost-effective improvement a homeowner can make. In addition to the drama and interest that a fireplace adds to a room, it can also provide heat in an area of the home that is most frequently used by the family, diminishing the need to heat the entire house. With an optional blower, the heated air can be forced to other areas in the house.

There are two types of fireplaces: custom-built masonry and prefabricated metal boxes. The former type is the most prevalent and by far the most expensive. The prefabricated metal box can cost half as much, since it doesn't require a concrete foundation or a masonry chimney, two of the most expensive aspects of fireplace construction.

A prefabricated box is easy to install in conventional wood wall framing; it is vented with a galvanized sheet-metal flue. The chimney is also framed from wood and can be covered with stucco or wood siding to match the exterior of the house. You can also have it faced with brick or stone for a more traditional look, although this will add significantly to the cost.

Adding a Wet Bar

A wet bar has become an important and useful part of the entertaining area in today's home. It provides a convenient and attractive place to store beverages, glasses, and other items used when entertaining. Most often found in the family room, a wet bar is also a popular addition to a den or study, a game room, and even a sitting area off the master bedroom.

A wet bar can consist of nothing more than a base cabinet with a countertop and sink, or it can include an undercounter refrigerator, a separate ice maker, and sometimes even a compact dishwasher. A more elaborate wet bar can also include open shelving above the countertop for storing glassware. An upper cabinet with decorative glass doors can also be added for more dust-free storage.

A peninsula-style wet bar is similar to a traditional bar, in which the host is separated

from the guests by the bar itself. Bar stools can be used with both configurations. Space allowing, cabinetry can be placed behind the bar for additional countertop and storage space.

The least expensive way to gain space for a wet bar is to install it in an unused closet or to encroach into an adjacent room. Plumbing for the sink should be a prime consideration when deciding on the location of the bar, since plumbing can be one of the most expensive aspects of the project. This is especially true if the wet bar will not be located adjacent to existing plumbing or if there is no crawl space below the house.

Adding a Family Room

Almost every home has a family room, regardless of what it is called. In some homes it's the living room; in others it's a converted bedroom called a den or a TV room. In homes such as these a family room can be a dream that is almost a necessity. The addition of a separate family room is the most likely way to return the living room or bedroom to its intended use.

A family room should be large enough to accommodate what a family needs to be comfortable when gathering together and relaxing. Options include a fireplace or a wood stove, an entertainment center or a big-screen television, a billiards table or a game table, and perhaps a wet bar or other built-in. An inventory of needs and activities will ensure the best design of the space.

Location is also important. The family room is best situated where the outdoors can be enjoyed through large windows or French or sliding glass doors with easy access to a deck, patio, or pool. Locating the family room near the kitchen is also a good idea, since the kitchen is a popular family gathering place. In fact, a kitchen and eating area that open to the family room provide an excellent large space for family gatherings and other entertaining.

Enlist the assistance of an architect, a design-and-build contractor, or a space planner to effectively plan a family room addition. These professionals

are familiar with building code requirements and can provide estimated construction costs.

Although it may be necessary to build an addition or raise the roof to gain a family room, the most cost-effective way is to remodel within the confines of the existing house. You may be able to enlarge an existing room by annexing space from an adjacent closet, spare room, utility room, and so on. You may also be able to convert a garage, basement, attic, or other auxiliary space. Sometimes the removal of a wall or two can give a room just enough added space to solve the problem.

Storage space is gained beneath the window seats and beside the fireplace in a built-in that also hides the television. New lighting and a refaced fireplace complete the upgrade of this handsome living room.

BEDROOMS AND HALLWAYS

Most of your time in the bedroom is spent with your eyes closed. However, that's no reason for you to close your eyes to the improvement possibilities of the room. The same is true with a hallway. You spend little time in a hallway, yet hallways are probably one of the most heavily trafficked spaces in the home. Hallways serve to link one space to another and have a tremendous influence upon what is anticipated at the other end. They're like the short subject before the major feature movie. For example, a long, dark hallway that has no windows or skylights may make the beautifully decorated bedroom at the end of that hall an unpopular place to be due to the unpleasant journey required to get there. On the other hand, a hallway with a skylight that reflects sunlight off warm, cheerful colors will act as an invitation to the bedroom beyond.

Small improvements, such as new wallcoverings, can have a major impact on the appearance of the bedrooms, and the hallway that leads to them. Large improvements, such as adding a bathroom to create a bedroom suite, installing a French door in place of a bedroom window, or adding a closet in a bedroom, not only add value to a house but make it a more comfortable place to live.

This bright, airy new bedroom addition features a window seat, tiled fireplace, ceiling fan, and south-facing skylights.

SMALL BEDROOM AND HALLWAY UPGRADES

Installing closet organizers is an easy, inexpensive upgrade that increases storage space and maximizes the potential of an inefficient closet. Installing mirrored closet doors—another small upgrade—creates the illusion of space in a cramped bedroom. Small upgrades cost less than $500 and can be completed in a day or two.

Applying Wallcoverings

By using patterned wallcoverings, you can alter the perceived dimensions of a room. For example, a wallcovering with a vertical pattern can make a long, narrow hallway seem wider and shorter. In addition, a wallcovering coordinated with the fabric used in a comforter or window covering can pull a room together.

Wallcoverings with light colors and subtle patterns or textures are the wisest choice. A wallcovering with a busy pattern can overwhelm a small space, and a dark wallcovering will absorb the natural light of the room, making it seem dark.

Select a wallcovering that is compatible with the other colors and finishes in the room. For example, a light-colored grass cloth would work well in a room that has hardwood floors and is decorated with earth tones. Avoid gender-specific patterns, which could limit the use of the space.

Like painting, applying a wallcovering requires careful preparation. The smoother the wall, the better the adhesion and the less apparent seams will be. Sand textured walls first to remove high spots. Heavily textured walls will require a light coat of wallboard joint compound over the entire surface.

After you have smoothed the walls, seal them with one coat of an oil-based primer. This will minimize the amount of moisture that is drawn into the wallboard or plaster when you apply the paste. The primer will also facilitate removal of the wallcovering in the future.

Adding New Lighting

New ceiling lighting is one of the most popular upgrades that you can make to a bedroom. No longer does bedroom lighting consist of just a single fixture in the middle of the ceiling. Today's lighting is an integral part of the decorating scheme. Decorative fan lights, recessed lighting, and track lighting are popular choices.

The most efficient design includes several switches, with dimmers, for controlling various lights. For instance, you might have one or two switches by the door for controlling the main overhead light and perhaps a fan. A switch by the closet can control the closet light.

Decorative fan lights are attractive and functional. By supplementing the heating and cooling system, a fan light is an energy-efficient addition that will pay for itself in lower utility bills.

Recessed lighting is as versatile as it is attractive. It is especially popular in soffits, dropped ceilings, and hallways where head room is limited. Recessed lighting has a variety of uses. The fixture housings are universal; the trim is what gives a recessed light its versatility.

A low-voltage recessed downlight with a small iris can serve as a reading light over a bed. Two such lights on separate switches are even more practical. The addition of a dimmer switch will provide mood lighting, which enhances the usefulness of the fixtures.

Wall-wash and multidirectional recessed eyeball lights offer an abundance of light in an interesting, nontraditional way. Eyeball lights are particularly popular in hallways to illuminate one or more pieces of art.

Track lighting is surface mounted and requires the same type of electrical wiring configuration as conventional ceiling-mounted light fixtures. A track light consists of one or more fixtures, called heads, which are attached to a rigid electrical track anchored to the ceiling. The heads are completely adjustable. Tracks come in different lengths and can be cut down or combined to fit almost any configuation.

Adding ceiling lighting to a room with attic space above it is relatively easy. The attic provides space in which you can install the electrical wiring without having to remove much of the ceiling wallcovering. In fact, properly performed, no ceiling patches are required for rooms where an attic exists.

To install recessed light fixtures in a room with attic space above it, purchase retrofit recessed light housings. Cut a small hole in the ceiling for the housing, and anchor the housing to the surrounding wallboard with the special clips provided with the lights. Run the electrical wiring in the attic and connect it to the housing before installing it into the hole. Install the fixture trim after completing the painting or applying the wallcovering. If retrofit fixtures are installed properly, no wallboard patches should be required in the ceiling.

If an attic doesn't exist and there are several recessed fixtures to install, it's best to remove all the wallcovering in the areas where the work will be performed. The steps involved in installing this type of recessed fixture may make this a medium upgrade. Purchase recessed light housings designed for new construction or for remodeling before the wallboard is installed. Such housings are meant to be attached to wood framing above the ceiling. Again, the trim is installed after the wallcovering is in place.

Upgrading Doorknobs

Replacing doorknobs is a home improvement that results in immediate satisfaction because it is quick and easy to do and because this seemingly small upgrade can make a striking difference in the appearance of a room. It's best to shop at a specialty store that deals primarily in door hardware; the selection found at home-improvement centers is usually targeted at the replacement shopper rather than someone who wants to upgrade. Be aware that top-quality door hardware, especially solid brass (as opposed to brass plate) or hand-painted porcelain, can be expensive.

Before deciding on the quality of replacement hardware, consider your neighborhood. The best return on investment in homes in modestly priced neighborhoods is from hardware with good-quality mechanisms and heavy plating, as opposed to solid brass hardware, which can cost almost 10 times as much, or light plating, which is only about half the cost, but which scratches easily and quickly becomes dull.

Replacing a doorknob is simple. However, since not all knobs are constructed exactly alike, it is wise to take the old knob assembly (including the bolt) to the store to ensure a proper match.

Fixing Squeaky Door Hinges

It's easy to fix squeaky door hinges so that the doors operate smoothly and quietly when they are opened or closed.

For years, sewing machine oil and graphite have been the lubricants of choice for door hinges, but neither is the best solution. Sewing machine oil attracts dirt and will eventually turn the hinge black. Graphite starts out black, stays black, and stains at the touch.

For the best results, lubricate hinges with an oil-free silicone spray. Many brands are available; some are labeled food grade. The product, which is odorless and colorless, can be found at hardware and automotive stores.

Installing Mirrored Closet Doors

Mirrored closet doors are a popular upgrade that are as decorative as they are functional. In addition to being more useful than a short mirror over a vanity, a fully mirrored closet door helps create the illusion of space that makes a bedroom or hallway seem much larger. A mirrored door also makes a room brighter by reflecting natural light.

Mirrored doors are available from home-improvement centers and can be installed by most handy homeowners in an afternoon. Most doors come with a head track and a base track. Both should be cut to fit the width of the opening. Attach the head track to the framing above with screws. Attach the base track to the floor framing with screws unless the floor is concrete, in which case use lag shields or wedge anchors.

Quality mirrored doors are a better investment than inexpensive ones; they have substantial frames that withstand

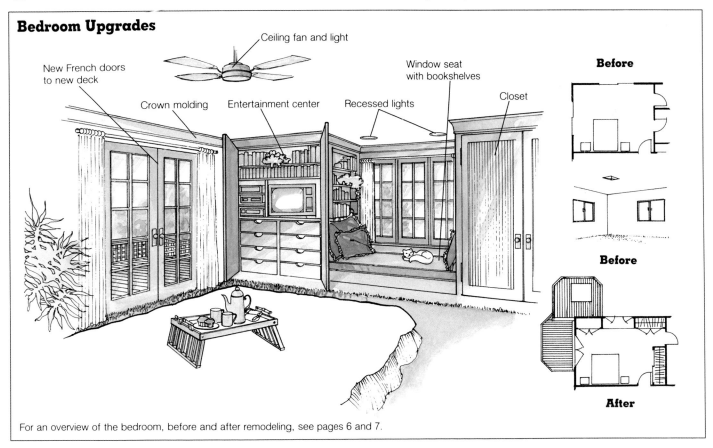

Bedroom Upgrades

New French doors to new deck

Ceiling fan and light

Crown molding

Entertainment center

Recessed lights

Window seat with bookshelves

Closet

Before

Before

After

For an overview of the bedroom, before and after remodeling, see pages 6 and 7.

Storage Ideas

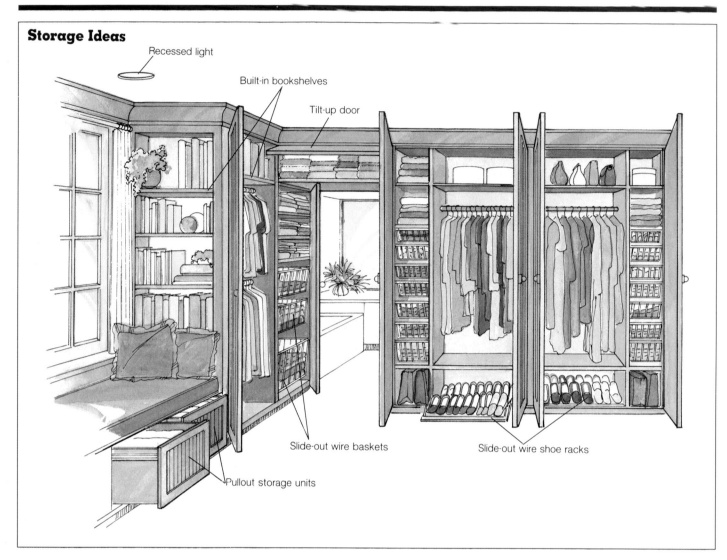

Recessed light

Built-in bookshelves

Tilt-up door

Slide-out wire baskets

Slide-out wire shoe racks

Pullout storage units

use and abuse and track systems with high-quality rollers that slide smoothly. One of the best ways to gauge the quality of a mirrored door is by its weight—the heavier the better.

Installing Closet Organizers

Insufficient closet space is one of the single biggest home-owner complaints. Most older homes would benefit from more wardrobe space, more linen space, and more space for coats in the entry hall closet.

Although additional closet space may seem to be the ultimate solution, closet organization systems are a cost-effective alternative that should be explored first. More often than not, the problem with closet storage is not insufficient space but poor organization.

For example, a closet that contains only one wardrobe pole and a single shelf above it uses less than half of the total available space. You can remove the existing shelf and pole and install a new system in its place.

Make a wardrobe inventory before installing a new closet organization system. This will assist you in designing the new configuration to best serve your needs. A double-pole arrangement (one high pole and one at a middle height) is excellent for short clothing, such as suits, sport coats, skirts, shirts, and slacks. This configuration literally doubles the space per lineal foot of area.

Adjustable shelving to accommodate items such as handbags and sweaters is an integral part of any organized

closet. Custom shoe racks will also help to tidy up the floor.

Prefabricated closet organization systems are easy to install for the do-it-yourselfer. Among the most popular is the ventilated, or wire-rack, construction, in which the wire is coated with white vinyl. Many of the hardware stores and home-improvement centers that sell these systems will also assist with the design. A wire-rack system for an average-sized closet can be installed in about a day.

# MEDIUM BEDROOM AND HALLWAY UPGRADES

Medium upgrades cost between $500 and $2,000 and can be completed in two to six days. Whereas many of these projects can be completed by a handy homeowner, some may require the help of a professional. For example, you may need to have a professional cabinet-maker construct cabinets, although you may be able to install them yourself.

Replacing Hollow-Core Doors

Solid wood doors have several functional and aesthetic advantages over hollow-core doors: They sound better when they close, they improve privacy between rooms because they are dense instead of hollow, they last longer because they are far less susceptible to damage, and they lend a look of quality. Although replacing hollow-core doors with solid wood doors gives a better-quality look and feel to any house, this upgrade is especially cost-effective for homes in medium-to high-priced neighborhoods.

Hollow-core doors, narrow trim, and inexpensive door hardware are just a few of the shortcuts commonly used to cut construction costs in modestly priced housing. All are easy and cost-effective to upgrade.

In most cases you can hang solid wood doors without changing the door frame, since the frame material used for a hollow-core door is usually strong enough to hold a solid wood door. You can stain rather than paint solid wood doors,

even if the existing frame is painted; this combination is considered acceptable even in the most expensive homes.

Pine doors are far less expensive than those made from other woods. If the door will be painted, pine may prove to be the most cost-efficient material.

Installing Glass Doors

In a first-floor bedroom, a sliding glass door or a single French door installed in place of a window allows more natural light to enter the bedroom and offers a better view. It can also invite the prospect of additional improvements, such as a small patio or deck just off the bedroom—a quiet place to enjoy the morning or to unwind before retiring in the evening.

The most cost-effective way to perform this project is to install a door that is equal in width to the existing window. In most cases, you must remove the exterior wallcovering surrounding the window in order to extract the window. You will also need to remove the interior wallcovering and the framing below the window in order for the new door to fit properly. If you have to relocate an electrical outlet, this is an ideal time to add a light

fixture to illuminate the area just outside the door. Such a light may be required; check with the local building department. In addition, you may need to add an exterior step.

Once you have installed the door, patch the interior and exterior wallcoverings to match the existing ones.

Although aluminum sliding glass doors are by far the most common and least expensive type, wood-sash sliding glass doors lend more elegance to a home. Most have snap-in mullions to create the look of a true divided-pane door. Wood-sash doors generally cost between 50 and 75 percent more than aluminum (which qualifies them as a medium to large upgrade), but with clad aluminum or vinyl exteriors they can be as maintenance free as aluminum. The result is a more attractive door with a slightly better payback.

The complexity of installing sliding glass doors makes this project a likely task for a professional.

Installing Built-in Cabinetry

Built-in cabinetry has become an increasingly popular feature in today's bedrooms. The uses are as varied as the designs and configurations. The most popular built-ins include the following.
☐ A full wall unit from floor to ceiling is ideal for storage of all kinds.
☐ A low unit beneath a window offers compact storage without interfering with wall decoration.

☐ A headboard unit combined with modest electrical features serves as book storage and a central location to control a radio and lighting over the bed.
☐ A freestanding divider can break a large room into more functional areas, perhaps a bedroom shared by two teenagers.
☐ A wall cabinet hung well off the floor is an excellent way to gain storage space without losing floor area.

If you choose built-in cabinetry that takes up a lot of floor area, it will limit the use of other furniture in the room, so make sure that this project is thoroughly planned. A good place to start planning any built-in is by appraising your needs for space and organization. Once you have established what is to be stored and how much space will be required, you can determine the cabinet configuration.

Although an architect or other design professional can draw up the design for a built-in, it is more cost-effective to have the design prepared by the person constructing the storage system. Even small cabinet firms may offer computer-assisted design. The plans produced by these systems are extremely detailed, yet are easy for the consumer to understand.

If you want to design and build the cabinets as a do-it-yourself project, start with a scale floor plan of the space. Show all existing windows, doors, and electrical wiring in the plan, so that you can integrate the built-ins into the space without creating any problems with traffic or furnishings. Next, cut templates of the furniture and the proposed cabinets to scale from construction paper and place them on the floor plan to determine how the room will work. Expect to have to try several different arrangements and configurations to find the best one.

Although this project is listed as a medium upgrade, it could qualify as either a small or a large upgrade depending on the size and complexity of the built-in.

Adding a Closet

If you have installed a closet organization system and there still is not enough closet space in a bedroom, it's time to consider adding a closet.

Building it into the existing bedroom floor area is one of the most cost-effective ways to gain a closet, if enough space exists. Most codes require that bedrooms have at least 70 square feet of open floor area, excluding closets and built-ins. Some local codes may require more space. You might want to consult a designer or space planner to ensure that this project will be an improvement in the long run.

The simplest version of this project involves adding a 2- to 3-foot-long nonbearing wall and installing a pair of bypass doors. You can create a more elaborate closet by adding more than one wall of varying length and installing a hinged door. This is also an ideal time to add a closet organization system (see page 90) and mirrored closet doors (see page 89).

Relocating a Closet Door

An inconveniently located closet door can interfere with the furnishing of a bedroom. For example, a hinged closet door that is located in the middle of a wall can prevent that wall from being used for a bed, a long dresser, or a system of built-ins. A practical solution to this problem is to relocate the door to a more convenient spot.

Moving the door a foot or so in one direction or the other may create enough continuous wall space to accommodate a sizable piece of furniture. You may even be able to relocate a closet door around the corner, freeing up an entire wall.

This is considered a medium upgrade due to the multiple tasks involved—rough and finish carpentry to frame the new door opening, seal off the existing opening, install the new door, patch the flooring where the new door opening was cut in the wall, and reconfigure the closet shelving system; electrical work to relocate an existing receptacle or electrical wiring, or to install a new receptacle and wiring; wallboard patching at the opening where the closet was removed; and paint touch-up.

Although this may seem like a complicated project, it is probably one of the least disruptive construction projects that you can perform in a bedroom; at the same time it is one of the most rewarding in terms of convenience.

Building a New Closet

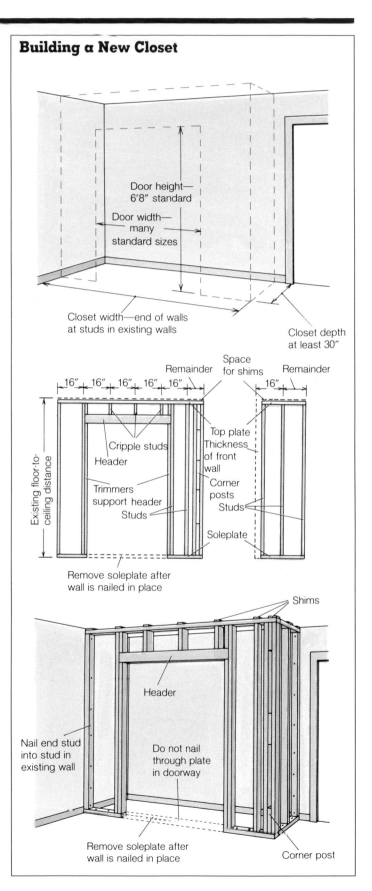

Door height— 6'8" standard

Door width— many standard sizes

Closet width—end of walls at studs in existing walls

Closet depth at least 30"

Remainder | Space for shims | Remainder

Existing floor-to-ceiling distance

Cripple studs

Header

Trimmers support header

Studs

Top plate

Thickness of front wall

Corner posts

Studs

Soleplate

Remove soleplate after wall is nailed in place

Shims

Header

Nail end stud into stud in existing wall

Do not nail through plate in doorway

Remove soleplate after wall is nailed in place

Corner post

LARGE BEDROOM AND HALLWAY UPGRADES

From adding a bay window to creating a master bedroom suite with bath, the large upgrades described here can transform a bedroom into a cozy, private retreat. Adding a skylight to a dark hallway can create a bright, airy passageway. Large upgrades cost more than $2,000, although some can be completed in a day or two.

Installing a Bay Window

Replacing an existing window with a bay window is an attractive way to bring more natural light and views into the bedroom. There are few places that one would rather be on a cold, rainy day than curled up on a bay window seat surrounded by fluffy pillows and engrossed in a good novel. At times like this a bay window is a perfect hideaway.

A bay window can also serve as a delightful place to display a collection of dolls or stuffed animals, making it the focal point of the bedroom.

Installing a bay window is considerably more difficult than installing a conventional window, primarily because it projects out from the exterior wall and often requires special framing and a roof. Bay windows that contain window seats must also have adequate underpinnings.

Most bay windows are constructed of wood, although some are made of aluminum. Like other wood windows, bay windows are available with aluminum- or vinyl-clad exteriors for low maintenance. Prefabricated metal or copper roofs are another option.

Unless you're experienced with these kinds of projects, installing a bay window is best left to a professional. For more information, see page 84.

Adding a Skylight in a Hall

In most hallways, which are interior and have no windows, the only means of letting in natural light is a skylight. It can transform a dark, uninteresting passageway into a cheerful space.

A 2-foot-square skylight is all that is necessary in a short hallway. For longer passageways, you may need to add a skylight at each end to create a bright space. If you need added ventilation, install an openable, or ventilating, skylight. It can exhaust unpleasant and musty odors and create a better air flow in summer.

In a house with a sloped roof and a central hallway (that is, a hallway that is not on an outside wall), the hallway is likely to be under the highest point of the roof. This necessitates a tunnel, or chase, that extends from the ceiling of the hallway through the attic to the roof. In most cases the chase will range from 6 to 8 feet in length. You can minimize the tunnel effect by flaring the skylight at the ceiling opening. For example, the opening at the ceiling can be 2 feet by 3 feet, tapering to the roof opening (the skylight itself) of 2 feet by 2 feet. For hallways wider than the typical 3 feet, the ceiling opening can be 3 feet by 3 feet.

To ensure an installation that is energy efficient, the entire perimeter of the chase should be wrapped with R-30 fiberglass insulation, from the ceiling to the roof, and the skylight itself should contain more than one layer of glazing. A double-dome acrylic-lens skylight with a bronze, anodized aluminum sash is a good choice. These are widely produced and hence offer the biggest selection of sizes and lens styles: clear, tinted, or opaque.

You must install adequate roof and ceiling support for the skylight in order to maintain the structural integrity of the house. In addition, you may need to relocate plumbing, heating, and wiring to make room for the chase. It is also important that the skylight be installed with proper flashing, which usually includes top and bottom saddles, custom fabricated by a sheet-metal shop, and step flashing for the sides. Due to the complexity of the installation, this project is best left to a professional.

Installing French Doors

All the details involved in installing a sliding glass door (see page 91) apply to French doors as well. French doors, which are usually made of wood, can give a bedroom an elegant look that is hard to achieve with an aluminum sliding glass door.

French doors constructed of wood are sold in a variety of finishes. Whereas wood is the most common interior finish, the exterior can be clad with vinyl or aluminum. Clad exteriors have become increasingly popular due to their handsome appearance and their excellent weather resistance. Clad exteriors are more expensive but are worth the added cost because of the ongoing maintenance and painting that wood requires.

French doors cost about one third more than aluminum sliding glass doors, due mostly to the initial cost of the doors in addition to the need for painting and hardware. However, the return is more than double that of aluminum sliding glass doors, because French doors are highly valued by potential home buyers. For more information, see page 83.

Building a Closet Addition

A closet addition is the best way to increase storage space if a closet won't fit into the existing floor plan.

One of the simplest and least expensive closet additions is a pop-out under the existing roof overhang of a one-story house. New construction is minimal: The existing overhang serves as the new closet roof, and using a raised floor allows the floor to be cantilevered rather than necessitating a foundation. A cantilever is also possible on a two-story house, but you should consult a structural engineer to determine whether additional support is needed.

Cantilever construction is used primarily on floors that are framed and where there is plenty of earth-to-wood clearance. With slab construction, which has no wood framing to cantilever, the slab is extended under the proposed addition and tied into the existing masonry.

Additions work best when the cantilever is 3 feet or less. A cantilever usually is not advised for larger additions, such as for a walk-in closet. This type of project would be handled just like a room addition and requires the same level of planning.

Among the considerations for a closet addition are setback requirements. The setback is the minimum distance a structure must be from the property line. These distances vary at different sides of the house and from neighborhood to neighborhood. A local building official can provide this information, as well as information about building permits, which may be required for this project.

Make an inventory of needs to determine how large the closet should be and how it will be organized. If other storage space is lacking in the house, you could make the closet addition large enough to hold linens, towels, luggage, and sporting equipment in addition to clothing.

Treat the interior and exterior of this addition like any other addition to the house—always match the existing finishes as closely as possible. This will ensure that the addition doesn't look hastily tacked on but rather enhances both the value and appearance of the home.

A closet addition alone will probably not be cost-effective; however, when combined with a bedroom expansion or bathroom addition, the relative cost of the closet addition will drop dramatically.

Adding a Bathroom

Bedrooms with a private bath—called bedroom suites—have become increasingly popular in order to meet the needs of the modern family. In fact, many families with older children or elderly parents living at home need more than one bedroom suite. The answer is to add a bathroom off an existing room. A likely place to look for bathroom space is under the attic stairs, if the bathroom door could open into the bedroom.

Since this project has become so popular, it is an improvement that not only makes a home more comfortable but also makes it exceedingly attractive to potential buyers.

For more information, see page 73.

Enlarging a Bedroom

The need for privacy, for work and study space in a bedroom, and for accommodating elderly parents are just a few of the reasons for expanding existing bedrooms.

The master bedroom in today's home has become a private sanctuary for relaxation and unwinding from a hectic work schedule. A sitting area with space to read, watch television, listen to music, or sip coffee in the morning is at the top of the list for master bedroom expansion projects.

Tract homes are notorious for bedrooms that are so small that a bed and a dresser are the only major pieces of furniture that will fit into the room. Although this may be tolerable when children are young, teenagers need more space—for a desk with space for a computer, space for a television and stereo, a place for books and other school-related material, and a place for hobbies.

If older or infirm parents should come to live in your home, part of what will make them feel safe and comfortable in their new surroundings is the ability to furnish their new space just as it was in their old home. Enlarging the bedroom and adding a private bath may be the answer. A couple of feet in one direction may be all that is required, or you may find that expanding in two directions is the only way to properly furnish the room.

Avoid creating a long bedroom. It will look odd, be difficult to furnish, and diminish the value of the house. It would be wise to enlist the help of an architect, designer, or space planner to assist you in the design of the room.

The process of planning to enlarge a bedroom is an opportune time to consider many of the other improvements discussed in this chapter. For example, if the enlargement will involve removing a wall with a conventional window in it, consider replacing it with a bay window, a sliding glass door, or French doors. This is also a good time to consider additional closet space, built-in cabinetry, and new lighting.

Combining several projects into one major improvement saves money in the long run.

Converting a Spare Bedroom to a Home Office

Making a spare bedroom into a home office is an increasingly popular upgrade, especially for people who must work at home because they have small children or want to avoid commuting. A bonus is that commute time is converted into time for added productivity, relaxation, or time with the family.

Although this upgrade may not bring a high return at resale, it can have a desirable and significant impact on your lifestyle. It usually does not require any structural changes to the space. Following are some suggestions on where to start.

Additional electrical outlets will probably be required for various electronics, such as a computer, fax machine, copier, and typewriter. If possible, put computers on a separate circuit to help prevent data loss. The outlets should have surge protectors to prevent damage to the machinery itself as well as loss of data due to power surges.

You will probably need to add ceiling lighting. The best office lighting comes from surface-mounted fluorescent fixtures. Recessed lighting and surface-mounted track lighting can also be added. For more information on adding a ceiling fixture, recessed lighting, or track lighting, see page 88.

You may also need to add telephone lines, one for a business telephone and the other to be shared by a modem and a fax machine.

Proper ventilation is a very important aspect of working in a home office. The proper exchange of air will make the space more comfortable for the user and will provide adequate ventilation for electronics, which generate warm air. An openable window or door, a vent fan, or an air conditioner for the summer months will make the space a more comfortable and safe place in which to work.

Privacy is important to make a home office an efficient work space. The need to keep conversations confidential and keep out distracting noise is of prime importance. Replacing a single-pane window or a sliding glass door with a double-pane window will not only diminish the amount of outside noise but will improve the energy efficiency and comfort of the space. A solid wood door in place of a hollow-core door will reduce noise infiltration from elsewhere in the house. Installing a threshold and weather stripping will further diminish sound transmission through the door.

For additional noise reduction, you can add a layer of ⅝-inch wallboard to the walls as well as to the ceiling if there are rooms above the space. This can be done only to the walls that are potentially a problem, such as ones that adjoin a bathroom, another bedroom, or a family room.

Plush carpet with a thick pad, and lined draperies will also quiet the space.

A built-in computer desk with pull-outs for a printer and keyboard can double as a writing desk in a room with limited space. Built-ins for books, manuals, and files are another added convenience that will help make a small room function well as a home office. Also consider replacing closet doors and shelving with built-ins or other office organization systems.

Adding a Fireplace

The addition of a fireplace is at the top of the list of home improvements in terms of cost versus value. Aside from the family room, the bedroom is one of the most popular places to install a fireplace. It makes the room a cozy place to spend time and unwind after a busy day. It can also add significantly to the comfort and energy efficiency of the room. With an insert, the fireplace can be used to heat an entire bedroom suite or bedroom wing of a house.

One of the most appealing aspects of this project is that it does not need to diminish the floor space in a room. The most economical way to proceed is with a cantilevered pop-out and a prefabricated metal firebox. This will require a minimum of structural work, which is expensive, yet will maintain the integrity of the house, both structurally and in terms of appearance.

Obviously, a small amount of wall space will be lost to the fireplace, but this can be a minor trade-off when plenty of other wall space exists.

For more information on installing a fireplace, see page 84.

Converting an Attic Space to a Bedroom

One of the easiest ways to gain additional space for a bedroom is by converting unused attic space. The requirements are a steeply sloped roof and a convenient place to locate the stairs. Converting the attic is an especially important alternative for homeowners who need added space but can't add on to the house because of setback requirements or lack of space.

An important consideration is whether the house can support the additional floor load. This and other pertinent questions can be answered by an architect, a design-and-build contractor, or a structural engineer. Because of the complexity of this project, you should consult one or more of these professionals to determine its feasibility, even if it will be a do-it-yourself improvement. See page 103 for other issues to consider when planning such a conversion.

The homeowners minimized costs when transforming a spare room into this library by using paint-grade plywood and inexpensive doors, but top-quality paint and attention to detail, such as the bookcase trim and faux finish walls.

UTILITY AREAS AND GENERAL UPGRADES

This chapter discusses improvements to the attic, subarea (the basement or crawl space), and garage, as well as general improvements not covered elsewhere in this book. There are many inexpensive, do-it-yourself projects that can add to your comfort or reduce maintenance costs, such as installing a fan to improve attic ventilation, using a layer of plastic in the subarea to reduce mildew-causing condensation on the subfloor, and increasing garage and driveway parking with a sectional overhead door. In addition, you can expand storage areas by building shelves in the garage and improve access to the attic with a pull-down ladder so that it is easier to store infrequently used household items.

The attic and subarea are also likely candidates for conversion when more living space is needed. In some instances these areas can be converted at far less cost than that of adding on to the house.

To give appeal to an apartment above a garage, and to make it a bright and workable space, consider skylights, built-ins, and recessed lighting.

SMALL AND MEDIUM GENERAL UPGRADES

Whereas in other chapters, home improvements have been categorized by room or area, some improvements are general in nature and can be made to every area of the house. This section includes such upgrades; they cost up to $2,000 and can take from a few hours to six days to complete.

Cleaning Oil Off Concrete

Oil leaking from a car onto a concrete garage floor is best kept in check with a drip pan, but accidents still happen. Once oil gets onto concrete, it can be tough to remove.

A simple way to clean up oil is with cat litter or sawdust and cola. Spread the cat litter or sawdust onto the affected area and press it in to soak up as much excess oil as possible. Next, flood the area with cola—any brand will do. Then scrub it with a stiff nylon brush, being careful not to let the area dry out. After about 15 minutes, rinse the area with water. You can clean the spot that is left with a solution of 1 cup liquid laundry bleach, 1 cup powdered laundry detergent, and 1 gallon warm water.

Replacing a Garage Door

By replacing a one-piece overhead garage door with a sectional door, you can maximize parking space in the driveway and allow a taller vehicle to park in the garage. Families with two or more vehicles, one of them perhaps a truck or a camper, will appreciate this improvement, which makes living easier and is attractive to potential home buyers.

A sectional garage door takes from 6 to 9 inches less overhead space than a one-piece door because of its position relative to the garage door header. Therefore, you may be able to keep some trucks and campers that otherwise would not fit into the garage out of sight when not in use. In addition, because a sectional door does not open out into the driveway but rather operates vertically, a car can be parked right in front of the door, which is handy if the driveway is short, if on-street parking is at a premium, or if off-street parking is required in the neighborhood.

Controlling Damage From Natural Disasters

In areas prone to earthquakes, hurricanes, floods, tornadoes, and other natural disasters, residents and prospective home buyers are concerned about how structures will hold up to future disasters. Upgrades that strengthen a home against these natural disasters are cost-effective from the standpoint of family safety as well as salability. In all but extreme cases, these upgrades can greatly reduce the chance of personal injury and extensive damage to the house. Such upgrades include bolting the house to its foundation, installing plywood panels on the cripple walls for shear strength, adding rafter ties, and installing metal connectors and diagonal bracing for post-to-beam connections.

Because the types of natural disasters most likely to occur vary from region to region, it is wise to consult local fire department officials for guidelines on how to upgrade, how to prepare the family to handle such a disaster, and how to deal with it after it has happened.

Utility Area and General Upgrades

For an overall view of this house, before and after remodeling, see pages 6 and 7.

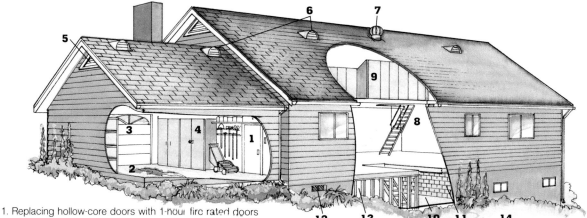

1. Replacing hollow-core doors with 1-hour fire rated doors
2. Cleaning oil off concrete
3. Replacing a garage door
4. Organizing a work space (workbenches, tool organizers, shelving, cabinets)
5. Adding eave vents
6. Adding rooftop vents
7. Adding a rooftop exhaust fan
8. Adding a pull-down ladder
9. Creating attic storage areas
10. Reducing water infiltration
11. Cleaning efflorescence off concrete and wood
12. Ventilating the subarea to inhibit condensation and mildew growth
13. Removing termite tubes
14. Eliminating wood and other debris on ground

Organizing a Work Space

A well-organized, well-stocked work space can make any do-it-yourself project easier.

Most avid do-it-yourselfers build a workbench before starting any other household project. A basement with full headroom is the most likely spot for a workshop, but you can even use a small garage if you have a portable bench or a bench that folds out of the way when not in use.

In either case, the bench should have a smooth, solid top. Plywood is acceptable, but covering it with a layer of ¼-inch hardboard results in a superior surface. Tiny parts won't get lost in cracks and knotholes, and the smooth surface is less likely to scratch what you're working on.

A well-organized basement or garage is handy, easy to keep clean, and appealing to a prospective home buyer. For shelving or cabinets, ¾-inch particleboard is the material of choice. Standard shelves are usually placed about 16 inches apart. Even in a small garage, shelving can be added above car level.

You can enclose the shelves by adding particleboard or plywood to make sides, using pine to create a face frame, and shaping particleboard into doors with a small router and two router bits—one to cut a dado and the other to shape the exterior edge. Knobs and hinges finish the job.

Pegboard is the most versatile way to hang a wide assortment of tools. For lasting quality and strength when the pegboard will be larger than 8 square feet, use ¼-inch pegboard. Otherwise, ⅛-inch pegboard is sufficient.

Every do-it-yourselfer needs a tool kit with certain necessary tools. Although the ultimate investment can be large, starting out doesn't have to cost a lot.

A good set of screwdrivers and a well-made set of combination wrenches, for nuts and bolts, are essential. Two crescent wrenches—an 8 inch and a 10 inch—are useful for odd-sized bolts and many plumbing fittings. For all types of home maintenance, including light plumbing work, channel-type pliers will prove to be invaluable. Having three sizes will provide maximum versatility—a 14-inch pair, a 10-inch pair, and an 8-inch pair. A finish hammer, a wonder bar (flat pry bar), a cat's paw (nail puller), and a nail punch will take care of the nail driving and removal jobs.

You will need an 8-point and a 12-point crosscut handsaw for rough and finish wood cutting, respectively, as well as a hacksaw for metal and a coping saw for sculptured cutting. A small block plane, a set of wood chisels, and a combination wood file and rasp will take care of notching and smoothing work.

A 25-foot measuring tape, a 2-foot level, a chalk box plumb bob, and a tri-square will make light work of measuring, leveling, and squaring each project. With the tools listed, you can make a satisfactory miter box from scrap wood.

An electric drill is probably the single most-used home-improvement power tool. Although one with a simple ¼-inch chuck will serve most drilling needs, one with a ⅜-inch chuck is a better investment. A sander will make painting and refinishing projects much easier. For making cabinets, furniture, and moldings, a router is a smart investment.

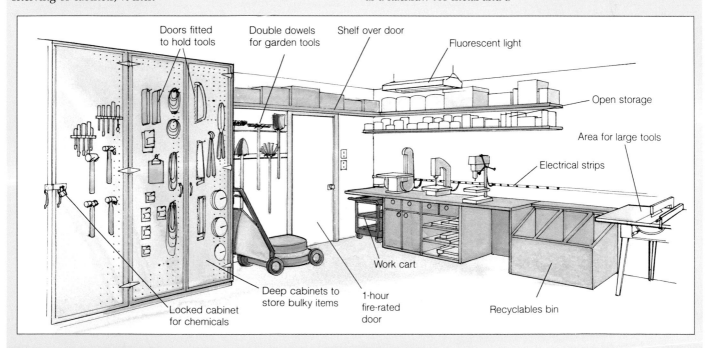

Doors fitted to hold tools · Double dowels for garden tools · Shelf over door · Fluorescent light · Open storage · Area for large tools · Electrical strips · Work cart · Deep cabinets to store bulky items · 1-hour fire-rated door · Locked cabinet for chemicals · Recyclables bin

SMALL AND MEDIUM SUBAREA UPGRADES

Subareas—basements and crawl spaces— are a prime target for water damage, from both surface water infiltration and from condensation. These do-it-yourself projects can prevent or inhibit such damage.

Reducing Water Infiltration

Surface water resulting from rain, melting snow, and irrigation can wreak havoc on structures below ground. Basements that don't leak are that way because the surface water is effectively directed away from the house at ground level or because the exterior surface of the basement walls and floor were waterproofed before the concrete was poured.

Because surface water is a major cause of leaks and floods in subareas, the abutting earth at ground level should be graded so that it slopes away from the subarea walls. Surface water will then flow away from the house, where it can soak into the earth without doing damage. You can also add a French drain (see page 22) to help keep water from entering the subarea.

The most cost-effective time to grade the earth and add a waterproof barrier is during construction. It is not practical once the walls have been completed and backfilled with dirt. Although waterproofing the inside surface is not as effective as waterproofing the outside in terms of stopping water, you can reduce moisture and humidity in the subarea with a coat of epoxy paint. Make sure that the walls are clean before you apply the paint (see the next section). Be aware, however, that hydrostatic pressure can sometimes be so great that even epoxy paint will not hold back the water.

Cleaning Efflorescence Off Concrete and Wood

Efflorescence occurs when water passes through concrete, stone, or wood and leaves a powdery white residue of mineral salts on the surface as it evaporates. When found on masonry basement and sunken garage walls, the residue is mainly an aesthetic problem.

To clean efflorescence off concrete or stone, use a 10 percent solution of muriatic acid (1 part acid to 9 parts water) and a stiff nylon brush.

Caution: Muriatic acid is caustic and should be used with plenty of ventilation, eye and hand protection, and protective clothing. Also, when mixing caustic chemicals, such as muriatic acid and lye, with water, follow the three-A rule of basic chemistry: Always Add Acid (to water). Never add water to a concentrated chemical—the reaction can cause splattering, fire, and even explosions.

Efflorescence on wood, especially in a poorly ventilated subarea, indicates the presence of water and the possibility of fungus growth. Using an ice pick, prod any wood on which you see efflorescence. Soft wood indicates that fungus damage is taking place.

If you find efflorescence but the wood is still in good condition, a simple cleaning-and-treating project can inhibit further damage. First, use a wire brush to clean away the mineral salt. Then paint the cleaned area with a copper naphthenate preservative that will reduce the chance of fungus damage. As with any pesticide, follow the directions and handle with care.

Inhibiting Condensation and Mildew Growth

Damp, cold soil in the subarea can contain enough moisture to condense in large quantities on the subfloor and cause serious mildew and fungus damage.

If the soil in the subarea is cool and damp, cover the ground in the subarea with a layer of 6-mil plastic sheeting, either black or clear. Lay it as flat as possible against the ground, and tape all joints in the plastic together with 2-inch-wide duct tape. Also use the tape to seal holes where penetrations have to be made around plumbing pipes and concrete piers. Any vapor that is created will condense on the underside of the plastic instead of the subfloor.

Condensation is less apt to occur when the area is well ventilated. You can simply add more foundation vents, up to double the original number.

Nail-on foundation vent covers are available that will fit most floor-framing members; confirm available sizes prior to cutting. To install a vent, cut a rectangular hole at the point between the foundation and the wood floor at the perimeter of the house. Use a drill to make a hole at each corner of the rectangle to be cut, and then complete the cut with a reciprocating saw or a handsaw. Do not cut vents in the supports below window and door headers.

Preventing Subarea Pest Damage

The best way to keep pests such as mice and gophers out of a subarea and also make it less prone to fungus damage is to spread a thin layer of concrete on the ground throughout the entire subarea. The concrete should be poured over a layer of 6-mil plastic sheeting (see previous section) to provide a moisture barrier.

This upgrade is easiest and most cost-effective in homes with full basements or at least sufficient clearance between the earth and the underfloor; otherwise extensive digging is necessary, making this upgrade costly and time-consuming. You can use a pump to transport the concrete quickly and easily into the subarea; then spread the material evenly and smoothly over the ground with a trowel or wood block.

For information on termite damage, see page 22.

SMALL AND MEDIUM ATTIC UPGRADES

Adding vents and an exhaust fan can make the attic and the entire house more comfortable by increasing ventilation. You can also expand the storage capability of your house by using space in the attic—for example, by adding shelves and installing a pull-down ladder for easy access.

Increasing Ventilation

During warm months, an improperly ventilated attic can trap heat, causing the rooms below to get unbearably hot. There are several ways to avoid this problem and make your home more comfortable: insulating the attic (see page 25), adding eave vents, and adding rooftop or gable ventilation.

Adding Eave Vents

In a house with a sloped roof, air enters the attic area through the eave vents and exits through vents located at higher positions. As air is heated by the sun, it rises and escapes through the uppermost vents, drawing cooler air in through the lower eave vents. This process of natural circulation helps to cool the rooms below. Adding more ventilation can help to improve the flow of air through the attic and aid in keeping the house cooler.

The best eave venting is found in homes with soffits (the panel that closes off the area at the roof overhang between the exterior wall and the ends of the rafters) with a continuous-strip vent. No improvement is needed with this type of eave venting.

Most homes have screened vents in place of some of the blocks between the rafters. Since these blocks provide some structural support to the roof, not every one of them can be replaced with a vent, but it is usually safe to double the number of vents that exist.

Remove every third block with a large hammer and a pry bar. You can then retrofit the empty holes with a screened vent attached from the exterior of the house with screws or nails. (Although the original vents are usually attached from the attic side, retrofit eave vents are made that can be installed from outside the attic.)

Circular eave vents are inexpensive and easy to install. Simply use a hole saw to drill the right-sized port into an eave block or a soffit and then attach it permanently with two small brads or screws.

Adding Rooftop Vents

Rooftop vents can be laced into the shingles near the ridge (peak) of the roof, the higher the better. There are two basic types of rooftop vents. The better of the two is the continuous ridge-mount type, because it is mounted at the highest point of the roof, continues for the full length of the ridge, and moves more air than the roof-mount vent. However, this type of vent is expensive, and installation requires soldering, making the job difficult for most do-it-yourselfers.

The other type, the roof-mount vent, is less effective than a continuous ridge-mount type because it moves less air. However, it is far less expensive to purchase, can be quickly and easily laced into the existing roof covering, and has no moving parts, making its installation maintenance free. Lacing in a new roof-mount vent is easy. A good installation results when the roofing paper overlaps the top of the base of the vent and when the bottom part of the base of the vent lies firmly atop a lower layer of roofing paper.

Adding a Rooftop Exhaust Fan

Exhaust fans help to drive hot air out of the attic. There are two types—motor driven (electric) and wind driven.

An electric attic fan is the more cost-effective of the two because it is thermostatically controlled, so it operates only when needed. When it is not running, louvered doors close and prevent rain and wind from getting into the attic. Although an electric fan is more expensive to purchase and install than a wind-driven fan, in the long run it is a better investment.

The wind-driven type of fan is a familiar sight to most—a round metal sphere with slots about an inch apart all the way around. The wind blows through the slots, turning the sphere and exhausting air from the attic.

The wind-driven fan comes in two parts (the base and the fan), which makes installation easy. First, you lace the base into the roof covering, and then you mount the fan onto the base. A rotating concentric sleeve is a part of the base and allows you to mount the fan straight regardless of the slope (angle) of the roof.

Wind-driven roof fans can be noisy, and they require maintenance. They should be lubricated once a year and should be covered in the winter to prevent water from getting into the attic.

Install a wind-driven fan only when your budget does not allow for the cost of an electric exhaust fan. A wise prospective buyer will know the pitfalls of having to deal with a wind-driven exhaust fan as opposed to the convenience and ease of operation of an electric exhaust fan.

Adding a Pull-Down Ladder

A pull-down ladder provides access to the attic and is easy to install. If you're selling your house, a prospective buyer will appreciate the convenience of this upgrade.

Pull-down ladders are made to fit between ceiling joists that are 24 inches apart. Installation will be easier if you can find a pair of ceiling joists that run parallel to each other in an area where the long side of the pull-down ladder will fit. Carpentry skills are important if alterations are needed to the joists.

Look in the attic to make sure that the location you have selected is not restricted by plumbing, heating, or electrical lines. It is also important to place the ladder in a location where there is at least 30 inches of headroom in the attic above the opening.

To build the rough opening, you must cut out the ceiling wallboard or plaster. The width of the cutout should equal the distance between the two ceiling joists (slightly larger than the width of the ladder frame). The long cut will equal the overall length of the frame of the ladder plus about ¾ inch.

Nail a solid block of wood the same size as the ceiling joist at each end of the opening, to create a four-sided box. The new end blocks should be flush with the edge of the opening. Then attach the ceiling material to the end blocks to hold the ceiling in place. Use three fasteners at each end. (Wallboard screws are best, even for plaster.)

Use cedar shims to fill the gap between the ladder and the ceiling frame. Attach the ladder to the opening with box nails (16 penny) or 3½-inch wallboard screws.

Finally, cover the gap between the frame and the ceiling with casing (trim).

Creating Attic Storage Areas

The attic is an ideal place to store lightweight items, such as luggage, infrequently used household items, off-season clothes, and sporting goods. Heavy items are best stored

elsewhere (see the next section), since ceiling joists are usually not designed to handle heavy loads.

If you want to store heavy items in the attic, it is wise to consult a civil or structural engineer about how to strengthen the framing so that it will hold additional weight. Sometimes this can be achieved with cross-bracing between the rafters and ceiling joists or by adding larger ceiling joists. Even if the floor of the attic is covered with plywood or floorboards, do not use it to store heavy loads without first consulting an engineer. Overloading an area with insufficient bracing can cause the ceilings of the rooms below to sag or crack.

Creating Below-Stair Storage Areas

Below-stair storage is an ideal place for items too heavy to be stored in the attic. Adding this type of storage is another inexpensive project that can make life easier and also add substantial value to a home.

This project, which might take two or three weekends to complete, usually consists of adding wallboard and a door. Since the walls below the stairs often support the stairs, it is important when installing a door to install a header across the top of the newly created door opening. The width of the opening should not exceed 3 feet, and the header should be a 4 by 4. The rule of thumb for sizing a header in a 4-inch-thick wall is 1 inch of header height for each foot (or portion thereof) of opening width.

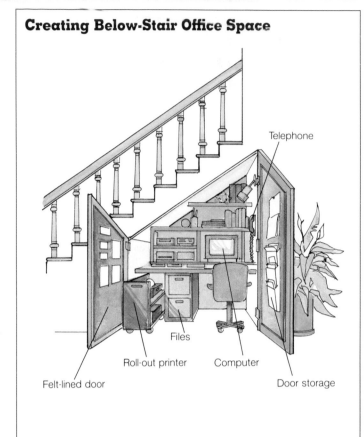

Creating Below-Stair Office Space

Telephone
Files
Roll-out printer
Computer
Felt-lined door
Door storage

Building codes dictate that fire-rated wallboard (⅝-inch-thick Type X) must be used on the walls and ceiling of the new closet. Although the wallboard need not be finished with a texture, it must be connected at all joints with standard joint compound and tape. This is called fire taping.

Also, all wallboard joints must be located over solid wood. This means that you must cut the wallboard to fit from the center of one stud to the center of the next. If horizontal joints will occur when the wallboard is applied, add 2-by horizontal blocks before applying the wallboard so that those joints will also be located over solid wood.

Use a solid wood door; it is more fire-resistant and takes longer to burn than a hollow-core door.

Why all the concern about fire? Stairs are the primary means of getting from one floor to the next in most homes. When stairs are not fire protected, they could burn quickly, trapping occupants on the floors above. This is the reason that current building codes do not allow gas-operated appliances, such as furnaces and water heaters, to be placed below stairs.

For information on how shelving can make closet space more efficient, see page 90.

LARGE GENERAL UPGRADES

This section addresses the issues involved in attic, basement, and garage conversions— deciding what makes the most sense for your home. Like the other large upgrades in this book, these cost more than $2,000, although some can be completed in a day or two.

Converting an Attic

Many older homes have large attics that were originally built to be rooms. Although they were left unfinished, they have their own set of stairs, dormer or gable-end mounted windows, and solid floor framing designed to carry the weight of living space. These attics are prime candidates for conversion to living space. Such conversions are more cost-effective than converting a basement or garage. When plumbing, heating, electricity, insulation, wallboard, and floor covering are all that you need to make the conversion, you can expect a 200 percent (or more) return on the projects.

The reasons are simple: The stairs, windows, and a structurally sound floor are the most expensive components in an attic conversion. Having any or all of these elements in place, especially the stairs and floor, add up to tremendous savings in construction costs. When stairs are in place to the attic, it usually means that the floor is built as a floor and not just as a ceiling for the rooms below. It also means that it is not necessary to alter the living area below to accommodate a set of stairs.

Converting standard attic space without stairs, walls, windows, or a solid floor is probably less cost-effective than building a room addition at the main floor level. Building stairs, adding dormers for windows, allowing proper headroom clearances, and converting a ceiling to a floor can all reduce the cost-efficiency of an attic conversion. However, when you need more living space and the house cannot be expanded elsewhere, converting the attic may be the only solution.

With any attic conversion, the design is determined almost solely by stair placement. Stairs should be located in a convenient and likely place—near the entry hall, for example, rather than having to be accessed through the laundry or a bathroom.

The best attic conversion is one that doesn't look like a conversion but looks like the rooms on the floors below. If an addition or a remodeling project is obvious, prospective buyers may wonder whether it was done correctly, if it will hold up as well as the original part of the house, and how much it will cost to make it match the rest of the house. It is important to match new finishes to old as closely as possible. Doors and windows, door and window trim, baseboards, wall finishes, and lighting schemes should all be similar. Angled walls or recessed or track lighting used in a converted attic but nowhere else in the house are a giveway to a conversion. If these features are used, similar changes should be made to other areas in the home so that all the rooms tie together.

Lighting, ventilation, traffic flow, and furnishability are other key considerations when remodeling. A good decorator, a designer, or an architect can be valuable in assisting you in these areas. For a sample conversion, see page 104.

This remodeled attic is brightened with skylights, track lighting, and a glass door to the balcony. The space beneath the eaves is well-utilized for bookcases.

Converting an Attic

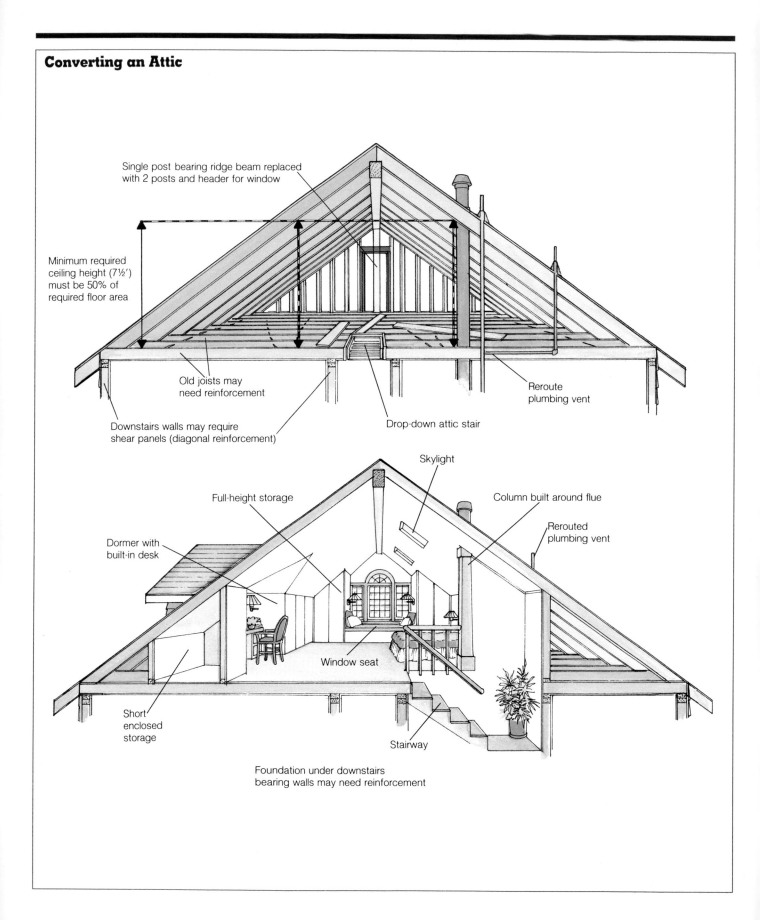

Single post bearing ridge beam replaced with 2 posts and header for window

Minimum required ceiling height (7½′) must be 50% of required floor area

Old joists may need reinforcement

Downstairs walls may require shear panels (diagonal reinforcement)

Drop-down attic stair

Reroute plumbing vent

Skylight

Full-height storage

Column built around flue

Dormer with built-in desk

Rerouted plumbing vent

Window seat

Short enclosed storage

Stairway

Foundation under downstairs bearing walls may need reinforcement

Converting a Basement

Converting a basement can be another extremely cost-effective way of adding more living area. As is true with the attic, stair location is a key factor. If stairs exist, the project will prove to be far less expensive than if the house above had to be altered to accommodate a stairwell.

It is important to know that stairs must be built to specific standards in order to be safe and to comply with the building code. Typically, the width of the stairwell must be at least 30 inches from wall to wall or to the inside of a handrail. The rise (height) of each tread cannot exceed 8 inches, and the run (tread depth) must be at least 10 inches. The rise and run of each stair element must not vary more than $^3/_{16}$ inch.

A stairway must have a handrail on at least one side; if the stairway is 42 inches or wider, a handrail is required on each side. These rules apply to all stairs, including those that access attics.

Some situations may exist in your home that make a basement conversion expensive or a poor decision. The most important one is dampness, which is not unusual with basements. If you have to use a sump pump each winter to prevent flooding in the basement, conversion can prove to be extremely expensive. Even minor dampness on basement walls is exacerbated when new framing and wallboard are added. Further, heating the basement can create condensation in new walls that will spur the growth of mildew, even if you use treated wood and water-resistant wallboard.

Another consideration should be natural light and ventilation. Basements that are situated partially above ground are the best candidates for conversion because windows can easily be added. It is important to have light and ventilation in a room, which may be impossible in a basement situated completely below ground level.

One aspect of conversion that needn't be of extreme concern is piping, ducting, and other mechanical equipment. In most cases these systems can be altered to create needed headroom, or they can be safely enclosed behind new walls.

If the basement is dry, if stairs exist, if windows can be added, and if the finished headroom will be 8 feet or more, a basement conversion can provide a 200 percent (or more) return on investment. See page 106 for a sample conversion.

Converting a Garage

There are only a few occasions when a garage conversion is wise. One would be when the layout of the yard and the layout of the house don't lend themselves to a room addition that will flow properly.

To avoid lost parking space, it is important to plan to build a new garage or at least a carport in the process. Eliminating the garage altogether can substantially reduce the value of a house. Although a garage is a premium in some cities, many municipalities now require covered off-street parking in all types of new home construction (including apartments). The era of car-filled streets is slowly but surely disappearing in American neighborhoods.

Although garage conversions generally are not cost-effective, if that is your only option for adding living space, the following suggestions may help.

Garage conversions that don't look like garage conversions, especially from the street, are the most successful. If you're thinking about resale value, remember that first impressions are lasting ones.

The owners gained a handsome bedroom in the basement by adding a bay window and using the foundation as a window seat and as the base for bookcases. Industrial-grade carpeting was chosen for its durability. The trim around the ceiling and window seat create continuity with the rest of this older home.

Converting a Basement

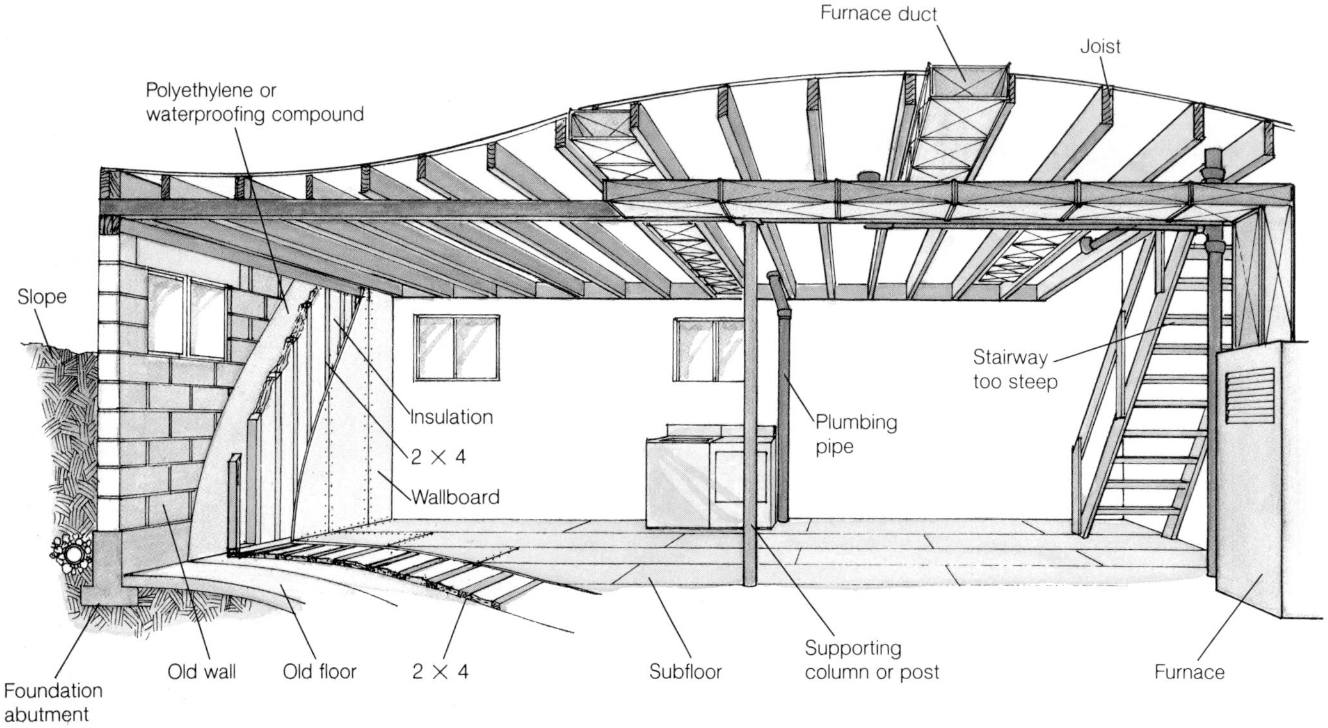

Furnace duct

Joist

Polyethylene or
waterproofing compound

Slope

Stairway
too steep

Insulation

Plumbing
pipe

2 × 4

Wallboard

Old wall   Old floor   2 × 4   Subfloor

Supporting
column or post

Furnace

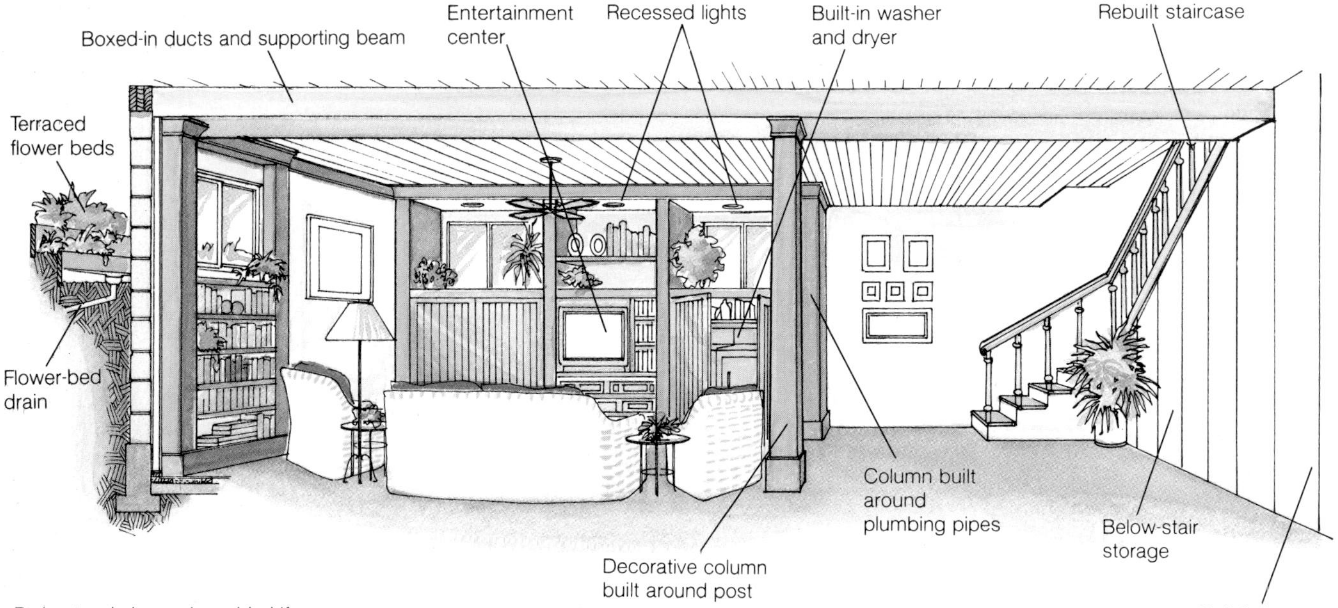

Foundation
abutment

Boxed-in ducts and supporting beam

Entertainment
center

Recessed lights

Built-in washer
and dryer

Rebuilt staircase

Terraced
flower beds

Flower-bed
drain

Column built
around
plumbing pipes

Below-stair
storage

Perimeter drain can be added if necessary

Decorative column
built around post

Built-in furnace

Avoid these dead giveaways: The driveway ends at the house and no garage door exists; no garage door or carport exists at all; windows are used in a layout that exactly matches the old garage door opening.

When converting a garage, it is important to alter the exterior so that its style matches the rest of the front of the house. This can be done with the addition of a popped-out roof, a continuation of the front porch, columns, soffits, planter boxes, shutters, stone or masonry veneers, walkways, and creative landscaping. Trees and shrubs can be used to break up the lines of a long wall.

On the interior, if possible, the old floor of the garage should align with the floor in the house. Ceilings should also align. Size is another important consideration: A two-car garage is usually too large to be converted to one room. A 1,600-square-foot house will seem out of scale with a 440-square-foot room at one end. The average family room or living room is about 210 square feet, the average second bedroom is about 120 square feet, and the average dining room is about 150 square feet.

If the garage floor is at a lower level than the house, it is a good idea to design an open wall between the house and the converted room in addition to installing a short flight of steps, since the steps alone would be a giveaway to the conversion.

Since it is difficult to convert a garage so that it looks like original living space, it is best to consult an architect or a designer to achieve a result that is aesthetic as well as cost-effective.

Top left: A closet in an upstairs hallway is a practical place to add a laundry area. Bifold doors conceal the washer and dryer when not in use.
Top right: Added storage is gained in this attractive enclosed shed, which avoids the cost of extending the roof and making structural changes to the house.
Bottom: A handsome, well-lit home office has been added in the basement of this home with a small addition, which allows for an angled skylight.

APPENDIX

Manufacturer and Contractor Associations

For a list of available publications, or for answers to specific questions, contact the following associations.

American Architectural Manufacturers Association
2700 River Road, Suite 118
Des Plaines, IL 60018
708-699-7310

American Lighting Association
435 North Michigan Avenue,
Suite 1717
Chicago, IL 60611
312-644-0828

American Wood Council
1250 Connecticut Avenue NW,
Suite 200
Washington, DC 20036
202-463-2760

Architectural Woodwork Institute
2310 South Walter Reed Drive
Arlington, VA 22206
703-671-9100

Asphalt Roofing Manufacturers Association
6288 Montrose Road
Rockville, MD 20852
301-231-9050

Brick Institute of America
11490 Commerce Park Drive
Reston, VA 22091
703-620-0010

Building Stone Institute
Box 5047
White Plains, NY 10602-5047
914-232-5725

California Redwood Association
405 Enfrente Drive, Suite 200
Novato, CA 94949
415-382-0662

Cedar Shake & Shingle Bureau
515 116th Avenue NE,
Suite 275
Bellevue, WA 98004
206-453-1323

Ceramic Tile Institute
700 North Virgil Avenue
Los Angeles, CA 90029
213-660-1911

Cultured Marble Institute
435 North Michigan Avenue,
Suite 1717
Chicago, IL 60611
312-644-0828

Insulation Contractors Association of America
15819 Crabbs Branch Way
Rockville, MD 20855
301-590-0030

Italian Marble Center/Italian Trade Commission
499 Park Avenue
New York, NY 10022
212-980-1500

Italian Tile Center/Italian Trade Commission
499 Park Avenue
New York, NY 10022
212-661-0435

Maple Flooring Manufacturers Association
60 Revere Drive, Suite 500
Northbrook, IL 60062
708-480-9138

Marble Institute of America
33505 State Street
Farmington, MI 48335
313-476-5558

Mason Contractors Association of America
17W601 Fourteenth Street
Oakbrook Terrace, IL 60181
708-620-6767

National Association of Home Builders (NAHB)
Fifteenth and M Streets NW
Washington, DC 20005
202-822-0200

National Association of Plumbing-Heating-Cooling Contractors
Box 6808
Falls Church, VA 22046
703-237-8100

National Association of the Remodeling Industry (NARI)
1901 North Moore Street,
Suite 808
Arlington, VA 22209
703-276-7600

National Burglar & Fire Alarm Association
7101 Wisconsin, Suite 31390
Bethesda, MD 20814
302-907-3202

National Concrete Masonry Association
2302 Horsepen Road
Herndon, VA 22070
703-435-4900

National Glass Association
8200 Greensboro Drive,
Suite 302
McLean, VA 22102
703-442-4890

National Insulation Contractors Association
99 Canal Center Plaza,
Suite 222
Alexandria, VA 22314
703-683-6422

National Kitchen & Bath Association (NKBA)
687 Willow Grove Street
Hackettstown, NJ 07840
201-852-0033

National Oak Flooring Manufacturers Association
Box 3009
Memphis, TN 38173-0009
901-526-5016

National Remodelers Council/Division of NAHB
Fifteenth and M Streets NW
Washington, DC 20005
202-822-0212

National Roofing Contractors Association
O'Hare International Center,
Suite 600
10255 West Higgins Road
Rosemont, IL 60018
708-299-9070

National Terrazzo & Mosaic Association
3166 Des Plaines Avenue,
Suite 132
Des Plaines, IL 60018
708-635-7744

National Tile Contractors Association
Box 13629
Jackson, MS 39236
601-939-2071

National Tile Roofing Manufacturers Association
3127 Los Feliz Boulevard
Los Angeles, CA 90039
213-660-4411

National Trust for Historic Preservation
1785 Massachusetts Avenue NW
Washington, DC 20036
202-673-4000

National Wood Flooring Association
11046 Manchester Road
St. Louis, MO 63122
800-422-4556

National Wood Window & Door Association
1400 East Touhy Avenue
Des Plaines, IL 60018
708-299-5200

Painting & Decorating Contractors of America
3913 Old Lee Highway,
Suite 33B
Fairfax, VA 22030
703-359-0826

Resilient Floor Covering Institute
966 Hungerford Drive,
Suite 12B
Rockville, MD 20850
301-340-8580

Sealed Insulating Glass Manufacturers Association
401 North Michigan Avenue
Chicago, IL 60611
312-644-6610

Stained Glass Association of America
63 West Street, Suite 7
Lee's Summit, MO 64063
816-524-9340

Tile Council of America
Box 326
Princeton, NJ 08542-0326
609-921-7050

Vinyl Window and Door Institute
355 Lexington Avenue
New York, NY 10017
212-351-5400

Wallcovering Manufacturers Association & Wallcovering Information Bureau
355 Lexington Avenue,
17th Floor
New York, NY 10017
212-661-4261

Western Wood Products Association
Yeon Building,
522 Southwest
 Fifth Avenue
Portland, OR 97204
503-224-3930

Owner-Builder Schools

Contact the following about classes and hands-on building experience.

Heartwood Owner-Builder School
Johnson Road
Washington, MA 01235
413-623-6677

The Owner Builder Center
2530 San Pablo Avenue
Berkeley, CA 94702
415-848-6860

Sacramento Owner-Builder Center
4777 Sunrise Boulevard,
Suite A
Fair Oaks, CA 95628
916-961-2453

Shelter Institute
38 Center Street
Bath, ME 04530
207-442-7938

Yestermorrow Design/Build School
Box 344
Warren, VT 05674
802-496-5545

Architect and Designer Information

AIA's *Beginners Guide to Architectural Services* provides information on hiring an architect and on the design process.

AIA
1735 New York Avenue NW
Washington, DC 20006
202-626-7475

Contact the following for information on interior designers.

ASID
1430 Broadway
New York, NY 10018
212-944-9220

ISID
433 South Spring Street,
10th Floor
Los Angeles, CA 90013
213-680-4240

Contractor Licensing Agencies

The states that are not listed rely on cities and counties, rather than a state agency, to license contractors and other building professionals. Check the telephone book under city and county listings for information.

Alaska
Occupational Licensing
 Division
907-465-2546

Arizona
Registrar of Contractors
602-542-1502

California
Contractors State License Board
916-366-5153

Connecticut
Licensing & Administration
 Division, Department of
 Consumer Protection
203-566-7177

Florida
Construction Board, Division of
 Professional Regulations
904-359-6310

Georgia
State Examining Board
404-656-3900
*Also city/county licensing,
except for plumbing, electrical,
and air-conditioning contractors*

Hawaii
Contractors License Board
808-586-2700

Iowa
Division of Labor, Contractor
 Registration
515-281-3606

Michigan
Licensing & Regulation
 Department
517-373-0678

Mississippi
Contractors Board
601-354-6161

Nevada
State Contractors Board
 of Nevada
702-486-3500

New Jersey
State licensing
609-292-5340
Also city/county licensing

New Mexico
Department of Regulations &
 Licensing for Contractors
505-827-7055

North Carolina
General Contractors Licensing
 Board
919-781-8771

North Dakota
Secretary of State, Licensing
 Division
701-224-3666

Oklahoma
Subcontractors Licensing,
 Occupational Licensing
 Service
405-271-5217
Also city/county licensing

Oregon
Construction & Contractors
 Board
503-378-3316

South Carolina
Contractors Licensing Board
803-734-8954

Tennessee
Licensing Contractors Board,
 Home Improvement Division
615-741-2121

Utah
Division of Occupational &
 Professional Licensing,
 Contractors Section
801-530-6628

Virginia
Department of Commerce,
 Contractor Licensing Section
804-367-8511

Washington
Labor & Industry, Division of
 Contractors Registration
206-586-6085

INDEX

U.S./Metric Measure Conversion Chart

		Formulas for Exact Measures			Rounded Measures for Quick Reference		
	Symbol	**When you know:**	**Multiply by:**	**To find:**			
Mass (Weight)	oz	ounces	28.35	grams	1 oz		= 30 g
	lb	pounds	0.45	kilograms	4 oz		= 115 g
	g	grams	0.035	ounces	8 oz		= 225 g
	kg	kilograms	2.2	pounds	16 oz	= 1 lb	= 450 g
					32 oz	= 2 lb	= 900 g
					36 oz	= 2¼ lb	= 1000 g (1 kg)
Volume	tsp	teaspoons	5.0	milliliters	¼ tsp	= 1/24 oz	= 1 ml
	tbsp	tablespoons	15.0	milliliters	½ tsp	= 1/12 oz	= 2 ml
	fl oz	fluid ounces	29.57	milliliters	1 tsp	= 1/6 oz	= 5 ml
	c	cups	0.24	liters	1 tbsp	= ½ oz	= 15 ml
	pt	pints	0.47	liters	1 c	= 8 oz	= 250 ml
	qt	quarts	0.95	liters	2 c (1 pt)	= 16 oz	= 500 ml
	gal	gallons	3.785	liters	4 c (1 qt)	= 32 oz	= 1 liter
	ml	milliliters	0.034	fluid ounces	4 qt (1 gal)	= 128 oz	= 3¾ liter
Length	in.	inches	2.54	centimeters	⅜ in.	= 1 cm	
	ft	feet	30.48	centimeters	1 in.	= 2.5 cm	
	yd	yards	0.9144	meters	2 in.	= 5 cm	
	mi	miles	1.609	kilometers	2½ in.	= 6.5 cm	
	km	kilometers	0.621	miles	12 in. (1 ft)	= 30 cm	
	m	meters	1.094	yards	1 yd	= 90 cm	
	cm	centimeters	0.39	inches	100 ft	= 30 m	
					1 mi	= 1.6 km	
Temperature	° F	Fahrenheit	5/9 (after subtracting 32)	Celsius	32° F	= 0° C	
					68° F	= 20° C	
	° C	Celsius	9/5 (then add 32)	Fahrenheit	212° F	= 100° C	
Area	in.^{2}	square inches	6.452	square centimeters	1 in.^{2}	= 6.5 cm^2	
	ft^2	square feet	929.0	square centimeters	1 ft^2	= 930 cm^2	
	yd^2	square yards	8361.0	square centimeters	1 yd^2	= 8360 cm^2	
	a.	acres	0.4047	hectares	1 a.	= 4050 m^2	